Introduction

This book supports students preparing for the Edexcel International
It comprises of 4 full practice papers. Each practice paper contains 25 questions and
detailed solutions.

The practice papers in the book are carefully modelled after past papers and specifications
of exam board to ensure that the papers as a whole provide a rich and varied practice to
meet all requirements of IGCSE mathematics with an appropriate difficulty.

Solutions are easy and comprehensible by people of all skill levels. They offer students
ways of dealing with common problems but also more complex questions that students
may struggle with under examination pressure. The solutions have been reviewed by many
students of varying skill, to ensure that they are easily understandable while being the
fastest and most re-applicable.

After completing these practice papers, you should be able to:
1. Quickly formulate optimal solutions to any IGCSE mathematics question.
2. More readily apply previously learnt skills on a question to question basis.

Contents

1	Paper 1	1
2	Paper 2	18
3	Paper 3	37
4	Paper 4	51
5	Paper 1 solutions	64
6	Paper 2 solutions	76
7	Paper 3 solutions	91
8	Paper 4 solutions	102

Paper 1

Materials
For this paper you must have:
- Ruler graduated in centimetres and millimetres, protractor, compasses, pen, HB pencil, eraser, calculator.
- Tracing paper may be used.

Time allowed
2 hours.

Instructions
- Use black ink or black ball-point pen. Draw diagrams in pencil.
- Answer all questions.
- You must answer the questions in the space provided. Do not write outside the box around each page or on blank pages.
- Do all rough work in this book. Cross through any work that you do not want to be marked.
- In all calculations, show clearly how you work out your answer.

Information
- The marks for questions are shown in brackets.
- The maximum mark is 100.

Advice
- Read each question carefully before you start to answer it.
- Check your answers if you have time at the end.

1   Find the lowest common multiple (LCM) of 10, 30 and 45

....

....

....

....

        Answer................................   (2 marks)

2   Find the highest common factor (HCF) of 15, 30 and 45

....

....

....

....

        Answer................................   (2 marks)

3   The first four terms of an arithmetic sequence are

    5   11   17   23

    Work out an expression, in terms of n, for the nth term.

....

....

....

....

....

        Answer................................   (2 marks)

4   Jack, Mark and Sam share some money in the ratio 3:4:5. Sam gets £15 more than Mark.

    Work out the amount of money that Jack gets.

....

....

....

....

....

        Answer................................   (2 marks)

5 Use algebra to show that the recurring decimal $0.\dot{2}0\dot{7} = \frac{23}{111}$

(3 marks)

6(a) Write 1.3×10^{-3} as an ordinary number.

Answer.............................. (1 mark)

6(b) Here are three numbers written in standard form.

Arrange these numbers in order of size.

Start with the smallest number.

3.4×10^{-7} 5.5×10^{-8} 2.1×10^{-6}

Answer.............................. (2 marks)

7 $\begin{pmatrix} 3+y & -3 \\ 2 & 1 \end{pmatrix} \begin{pmatrix} -2 \\ x \end{pmatrix} = \begin{pmatrix} -8 \\ 2 \end{pmatrix}$

Find the value of x and the value of y.

Answer.............................. (2 marks)

8 In Hong Kong, Alice bought 4 boxes of chocolate, each costing 52 HKD (Hong Kong Dollars). Alice also bought 2 watches, each costing 450 HKD.

The exchange rate was £1=11.85 HKD.

Calculate the total cost of these six items, in £, to the nearest pound.

....

....

....

....

....

....

....

Answer................................   (3 marks)

9 Without using a calculator, evaluate $\dfrac{\sqrt{72}-\sqrt{32}}{\sqrt{50}}$

....

....

....

....

....

....

Answer................................   (2 marks)

10 a, b, c and d are four integers.

Their mean is 9.5, their mode is 8, and their median is 9.

10(a) Find the value of the largest of the four integers.

....

....

....

....

....

Answer................................   (3 marks)

10(b) Find the mean value of the numbers (3*a*-4), (3*b*-4), (3*c*-4) and (3*d*-4).

Answer.............................. (2 marks)

11(a) Write $2x^2 - 8x + 5$ in the form $a(x+b)^2 + c$

Answer.............................. (3 marks)

11(b) Line *L* is the line of symmetry of the curve with equation $y = 2x^2 - 8x + 5$

Using your answer to part (a) or otherwise, work out the equation of *L*.

Answer.............................. (3 marks)

12 *P* is inversely proportional to Q^2 where $Q > 0$. $P = 100$ when $Q = 6$.

Find the value of *Q* when $P = 16$.

Answer.............................. (3 marks)

13    $A=\{2, 3, 4, 6, 8, 10, 12, 14\}$, $B=\{3, 6, 9, 10\}$. List the members of the set.

13(a) $A \cup B$

....
....
....
....
....

    Answer............................   (3 marks)

13(b) $A \cap B$

....
....
....
....
....

    Answer............................   (3 marks)

14    $y = \dfrac{3a}{2b-c}$

$a = 43$ correct to 2 significant figures.

$b = 26$ correct to 2 significant figures.

$c = 32$ correct to 2 significant figures.

Work out the lower bound for the value of y.

Give your answer correct to 2 significant figures.

Show your working clearly.

....
....
....
....
....
....

    Answer............................   (4 marks)

15   *ABC* is a right-angled triangle. ∠*B* = 90°, ∠*A* = 40°, *AC* = 18 cm. Calculate the length of *BC*.

Give your answer to 3 significant figures.

Diagram **NOT** accurately drawn

Answer.................................   (3 marks)

16 The regular pentagon *ABCDE* is drawn inside the regular octagon *ABFGHIJK*.

They share side *AB*.

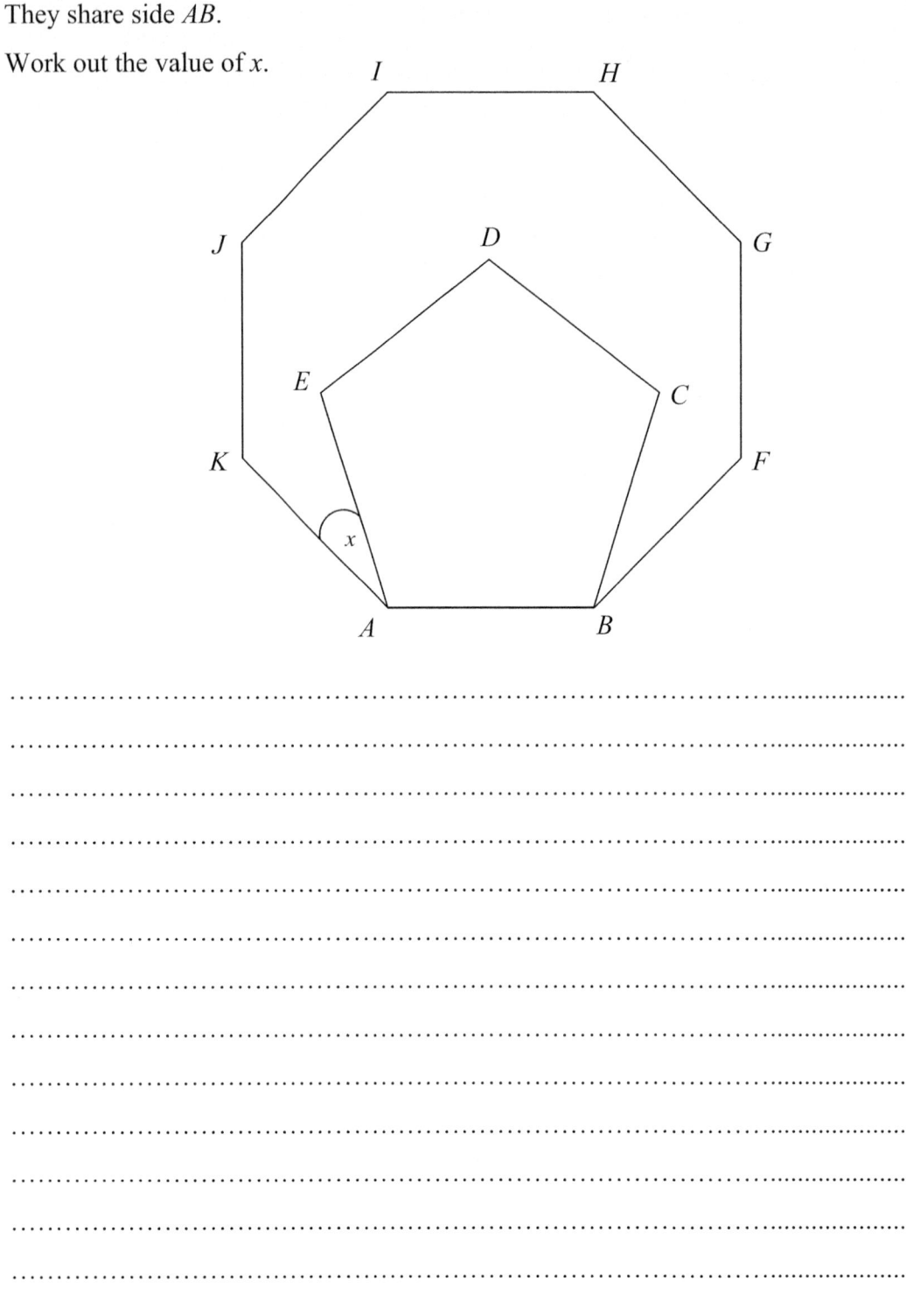

Work out the value of *x*.

Answer.................................. (3 marks)

17 ABCD are on the circumference of a circle. AE is a tangent to the circle.

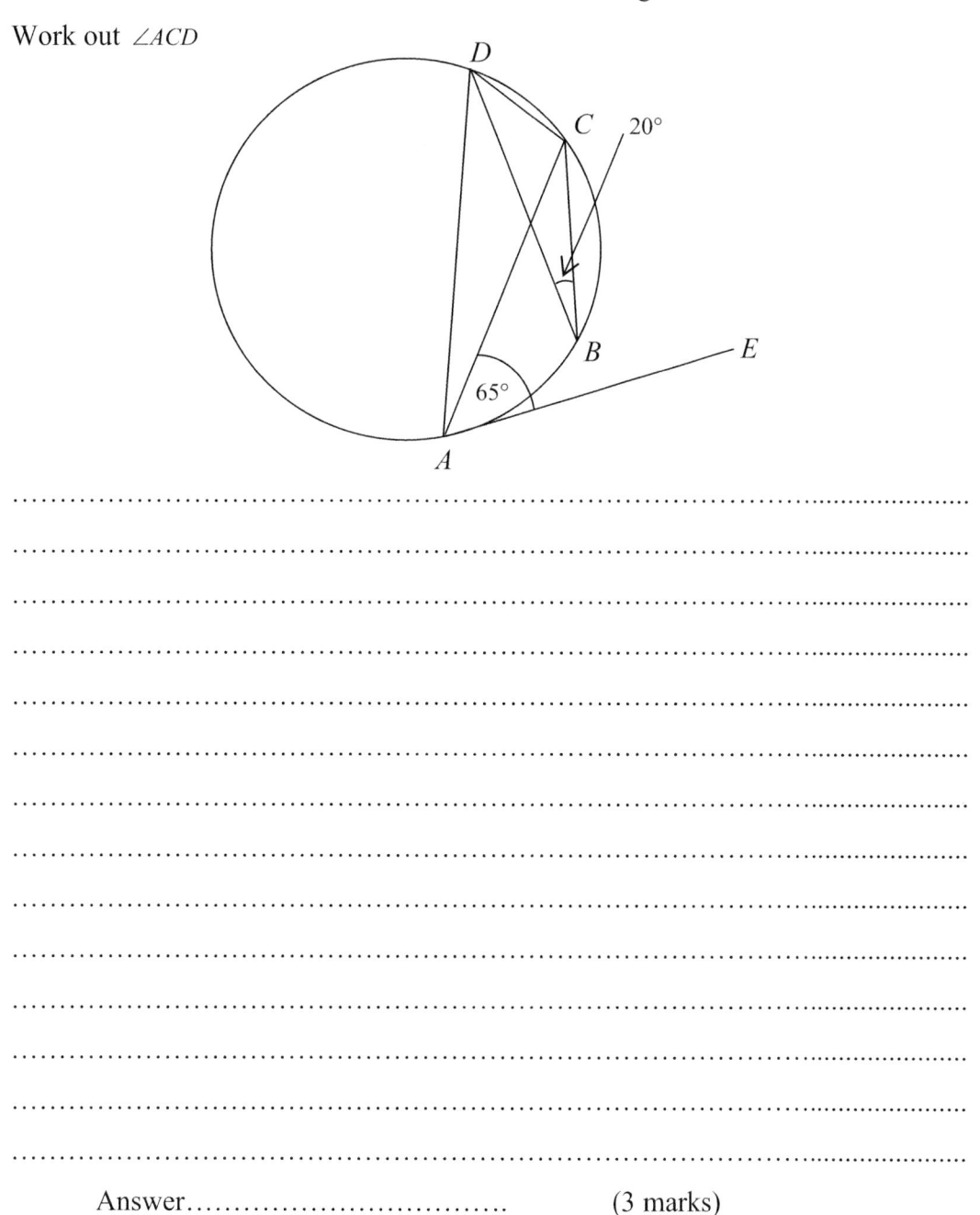

Work out ∠ACD

Answer…………………………….   (3 marks)

18 The table shows information about the height of some plants.

Height (cm)	$0 < h \leq 20$	$20 < h \leq 30$	$30 < h \leq 40$	$40 < h \leq 70$
Number of plants	24	38	33	30

The histogram for the height of less than 20 cm of the plants is drawn on the graph.

Complete the histogram for this information.

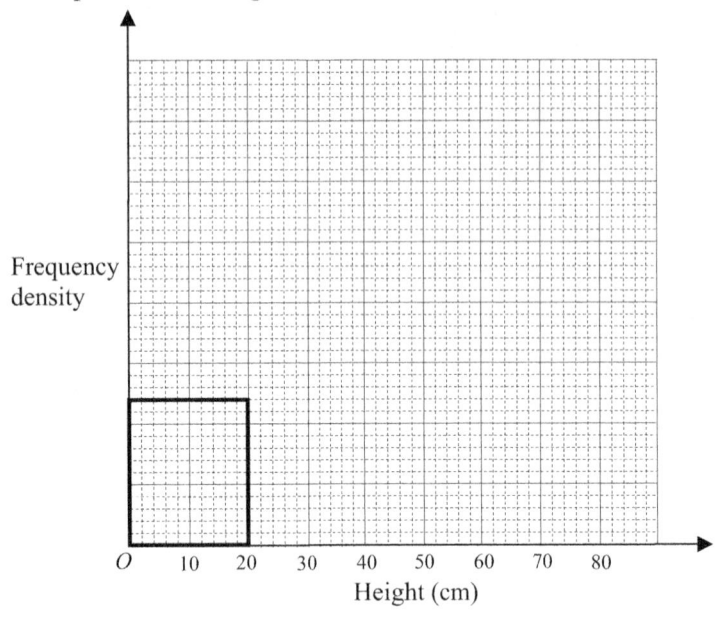

(3 marks)

19 Emma and Jack race against each other in a competition. The probability that Emma wins is 0.6 each time. A draw is not possible. They run two races.

19(a) Complete and fully label the probability tree diagram to show the possible outcome.

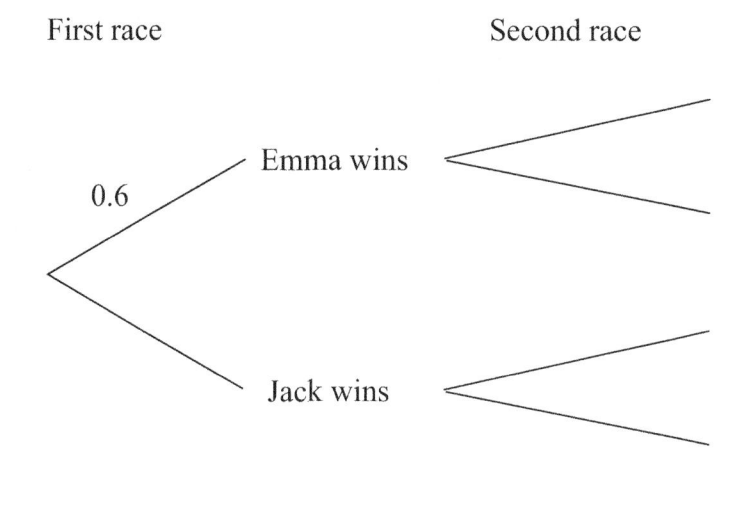

First race   Second race

0.6 → Emma wins

Jack wins

(4 marks)

19(b) Calculate the probability that each of them wins only one race.

Answer………………………. (3 marks)

20 The points *O, A, B* and *C* are such that

$\vec{OA} = \begin{pmatrix} 1 \\ 1 \end{pmatrix}$ $\vec{AB} = \begin{pmatrix} 3 \\ 2 \end{pmatrix}$ $\vec{OC} = \begin{pmatrix} 5 \\ 6 \end{pmatrix}$

Find $\vec{BC}$ as a column vector

Answer………………………. (3 marks)

10

11

21 *A* is the point with coordinates (-3,2) and *B* is the point with coordinates (13,10).

21(a) Calculate the gradient of the straight line *AB*.

....

....

....

Answer………………………. (3 marks)

21(b) Calculate the length of *AB*.

Give your answer to 1 decimal place.

....

....

....

Answer………………………. (3 marks)

22   On the grid below indicate clearly the region R defined by the three inequalities.

$x \leq 2$

$y \leq x+3$

$y \geq -x-3$

22(a) Label the region clearly with an R.

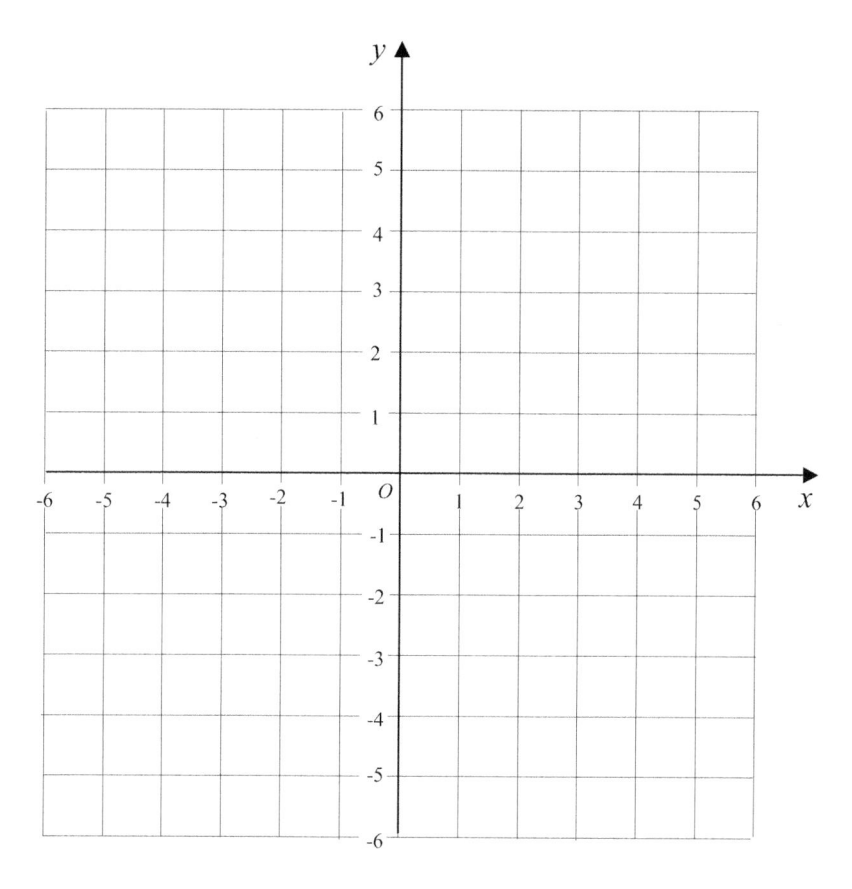

(3 marks)

22(b) Calculate the area of the region R.

....

....

....

....

....

....

Answer................................   (3 marks)

23(a) Describe fully the single transformation that maps triangle **P** onto triangle **Q**.

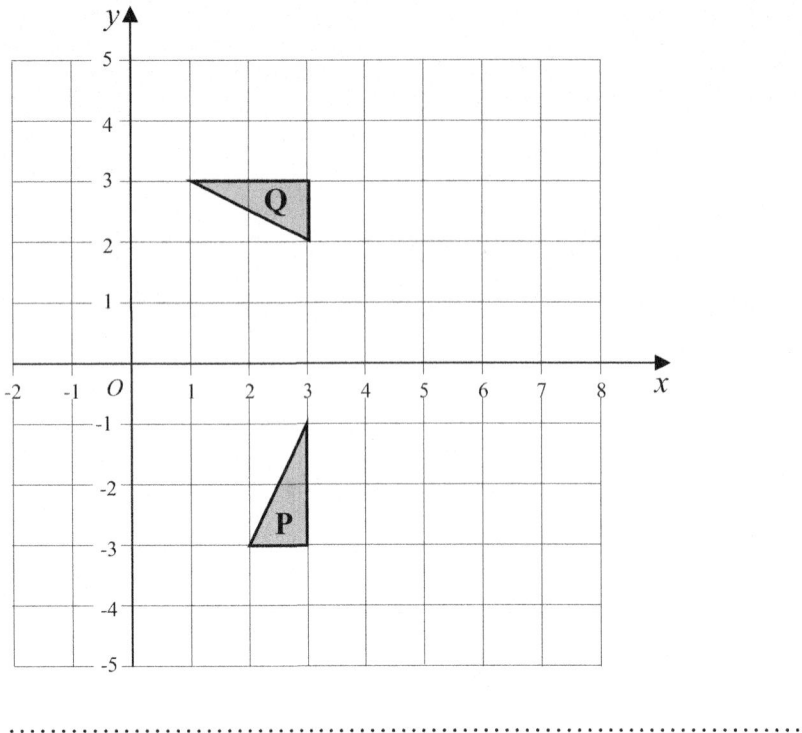

....
....
....
....

Answer............................... (3 marks)

23(b) On the grid, translate triangle **P** 4 squares to the right and 5 squares up. Label the new triangle **R**.

....
....
....

(3 marks)

24 The diagram shows the graph of $y = \sin x$ for $0° \leq x \leq 360°$

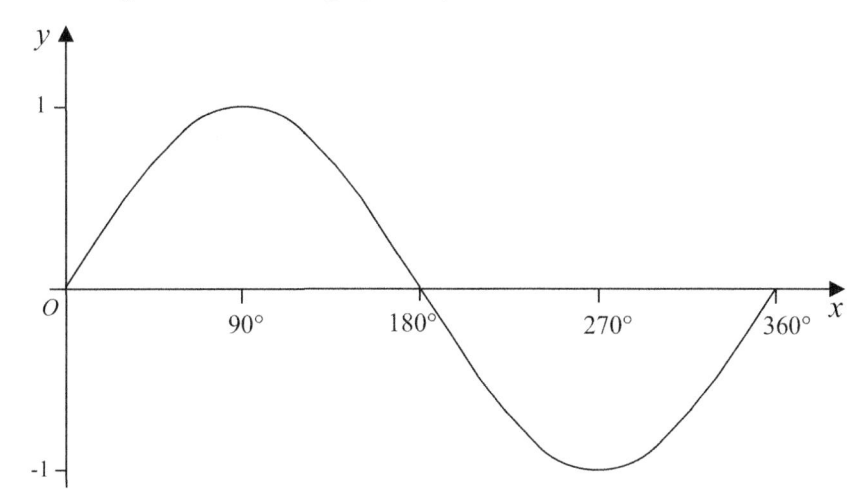

The two diagrams below show the graphs of transformations of $y = \sin x$

Write down the equation of each graph.

24(a)

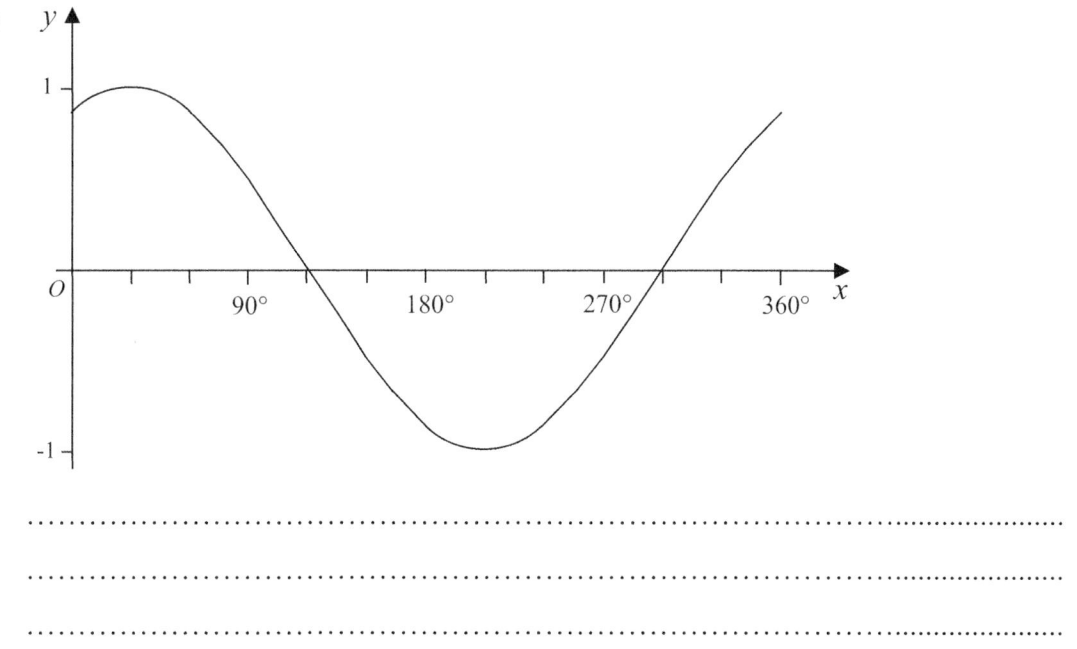

....
....
....

Answer.............................. (3 marks)

24(b)

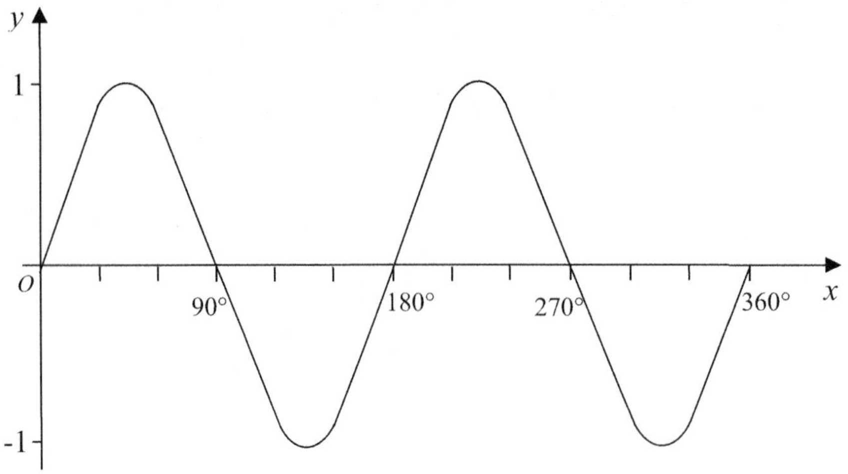

....

....

....

Answer.................................. (3 marks)

25 The diagram shows parts of the graph of $y = f(x)$ and $y = g(x)$.

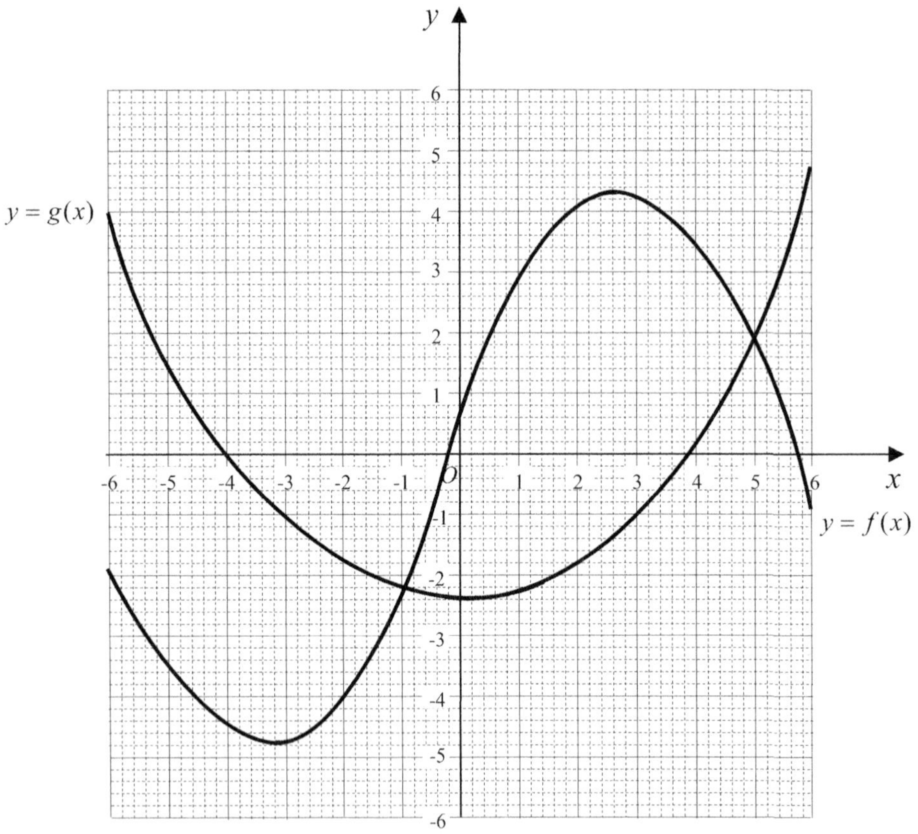

3

25(a) Find $g(3)$

....
....
....
....
....

Answer................................ (3 marks)

25(b) Find $gf(-2)$

....
....
....
....
....

Answer................................ (3 marks)

25(c) Calculate an estimate for the gradient of the curve $y = f(x)$ at the point on the curve where $x = -2$.

....
....
....
....
....

Answer................................ (3 marks)

Paper 2

Materials

For this paper you must have:
- Ruler graduated in centimetres and millimetres, protractor, compasses, pen, HB pencil, eraser, calculator.
- Tracing paper may be used.

Time allowed

2 hours.

Instructions
- Use black ink or black ball-point pen. Draw diagrams in pencil.
- Answer all questions.
- You must answer the questions in the space provided. Do not write outside the box around each page or on blank pages.
- Do all rough work in this book. Cross through any work that you do not want to be marked.
- In all calculations, show clearly how you work out your answer.

Information
- The marks for questions are shown in brackets.
- The maximum mark is 100.

Advice
- Read each question carefully before you start to answer it.
- Check your answers if you have time at the end.

1   Expand $(3+2\sqrt{3})^2$

Give your answer in the form $a+b\sqrt{3}$, where a and b are integers.

Show your working clearly.

Answer................................. (2 marks)

2   Simplify the expression $(2x^3y^2)^4$

Answer................................. (2 marks)

3   Solve the simultaneous equations

$2x+y=13$

$x-y=8$

Answer................................. (2 marks)

4   Show, using algebra, that the sum of any 4 consecutive integers is always even.

Answer................................. (2 marks)

5(a) $x^2 - 4x - 12 \leq 0$

Work out the range of values of x

....
....
....

Answer................................ (2 marks)

5(b) Solve $x^4 = 4x^2$

....
....
....

Answer................................ (3 marks)

6 A bag contains blue, green and white balls. The ratio of blue balls to green balls is 2:3. The ratio of green balls to white balls is 2:5.

Work out the smallest possible number of balls in the bag.

....
....
....
....
....

Answer................................ (3 marks)

7 Sarah flew on a plane from Beijing to London.

The plane flew a distance of 8400 km.

The flight time was 10 hours and 15 minutes.

Work out the average speed of the plane in kilometres per hour.

Give your answer to 1 decimal place.

....
....
....
....

Answer................................ (2 marks)

8   An antiques dealer buys a vase for £400. He sells the vase for 50% more than the price he paid for it.

8(a)   For how much does the dealer sell the vase?

....
....
....
....

Answer................................   (2 marks)

8(b)   It costs the dealer £60 to restore the vase before he sell it. Calculate the amount of profit the deal made.

....
....
....

Answer................................   (3 marks)

8(c)   Calculate this profit as a percentage of the price the dealer paid for the vase.

....
....
....

Answer................................   (2 marks)

9 P is directly proportional to Q^2 where $Q > 0$. $P = 900$ when $Q = 15$.

9(a) Find a formula for P in terms of Q.

Answer.................................. (2 marks)

9(b) Find the value of Q when $P = 25$.

Answer.................................. (2 marks)

10 Rearrange $y = \sqrt[3]{\dfrac{2(w-x)}{x}}$ to make x the subject.

Answer.................................. (3 marks)

11   Solid **A** and Solid **B** are mathematically similar.

Solid **A** has a volume of 728 cm³

Solid **B** has a volume of 5824 cm³

Solid **A** has surface area 384 cm²

Calculate the surface area of solid **B**.

....

....

....

....

....

....

Answer……………………………….   (3 marks)

12   $f(x) = \dfrac{1}{\sqrt{x+3}}$

12(a) State the range of values of x which must be excluded from the domain of $f(x)$

....

....

....

....

....

....

....

Answer……………………………….   (3 marks)

12(b) $g(x) = 3x$

Calculate $fg(2)$

....

....

....

....

....

Answer……………………………….   (3 marks)

13(a) A cuboid has the following dimensions:

Length 250 mm, measured to the nearest 10 mm

Breadth 150 mm, measured to the nearest 10 mm

Height 60 mm, measured to the nearest 10 mm.

Calculate the greatest possible volume of the cuboid.

Answer............................... (3 marks)

13(b) Another cuboid has a volume of 20000 mm^3, measured to the nearest 100 mm^3. The area of its base (length × breadth) is 120 mm^2, measured to the nearest 10 mm^2. Calculate the smallest possible height of this cuboid.

Give your answer to 3 significant figures.

Answer............................... (3 marks)

14 ABCD is a kite.

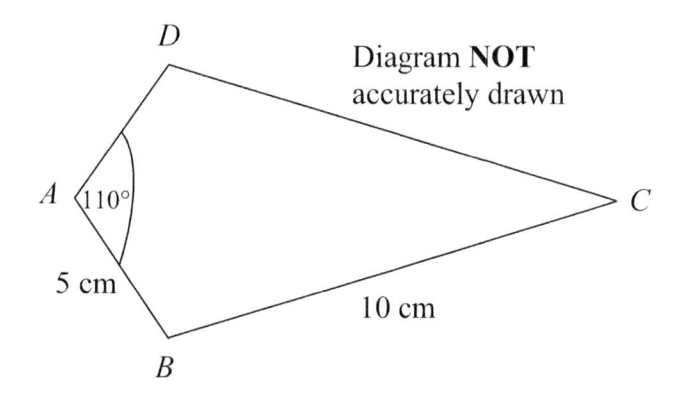

Diagram **NOT** accurately drawn

$AB = 5$ cm, $BC = 10$ cm, $\angle BAD = 110°$

Calculate the area of kite ABCD.

Give your answer to 3 significant figures.

....

....

....

....

....

....

....

....

....

....

Answer……………………….   (3 marks)

15 The tent shown in the diagram has a base that is 2.5 m wide and 4.0 m long. The height of the tent is 1.5 m. The ends are isosceles triangles *AE = ED*, *BF = FC*, and perpendicular to the base.

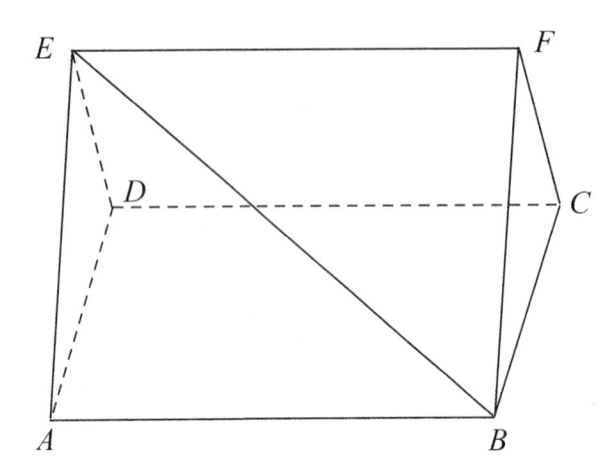

15(a) Work out the length of *BE*.

Give your answer to 3 significant figures.

....
....
....
....
....

Answer............................... (3 marks)

15(b) Work out the angle between *BE* and *ABCD*.

Give your answer to 1 decimal place.

....
....
....
....
....

Answer............................... (3 marks)

16 The diagram shows a regular pentagon *ABCDE*. The perimeter of the pentagon is 50 cm.

Calculate the area of the pentagon.

Give your answer to 2 decimal places.

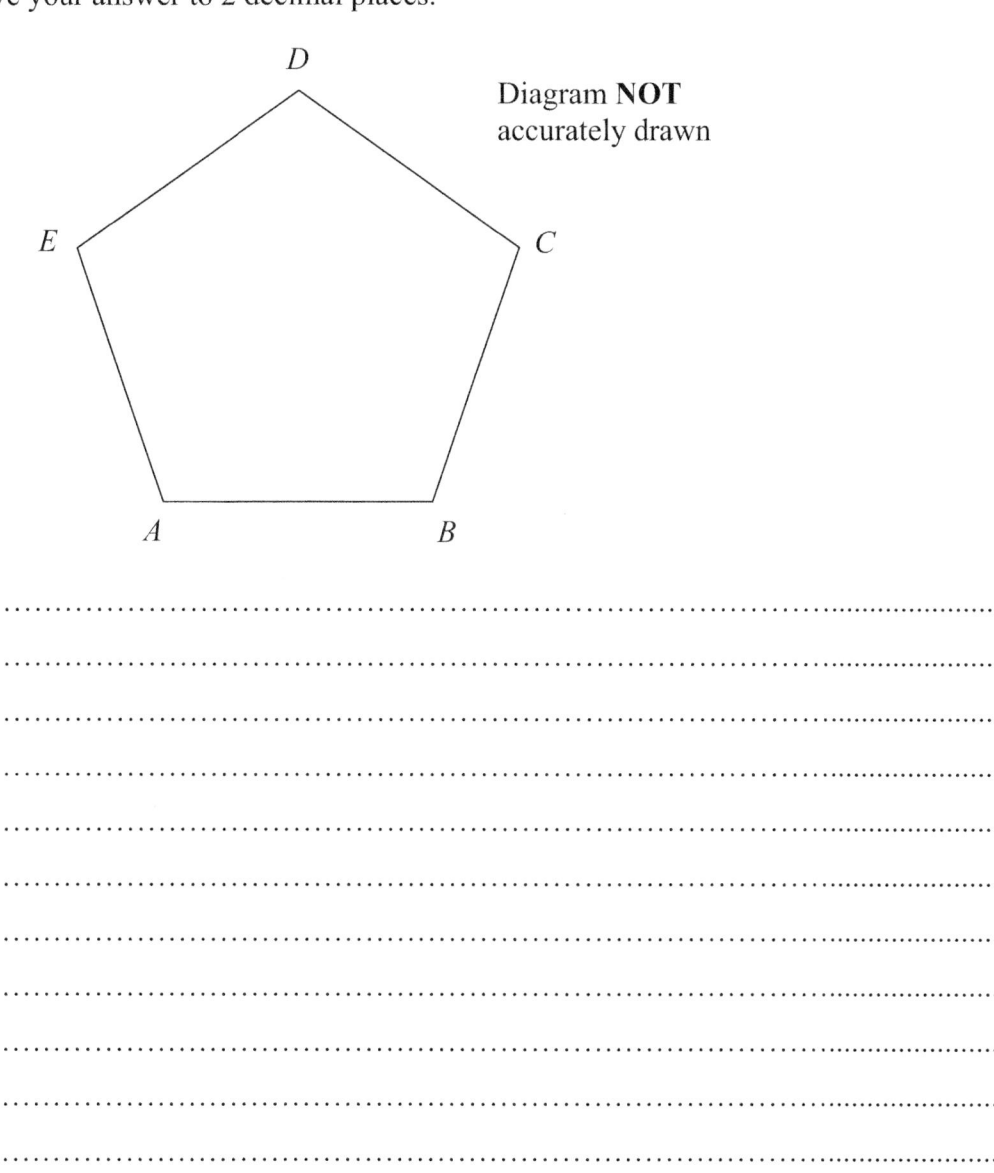

Diagram **NOT** accurately drawn

Answer.............................. (3 marks)

17 *ABCD* is a cyclic quadrilateral. ∠*DAB* = 2 × ∠*CDT*, *DT* is a tangent to the circle.

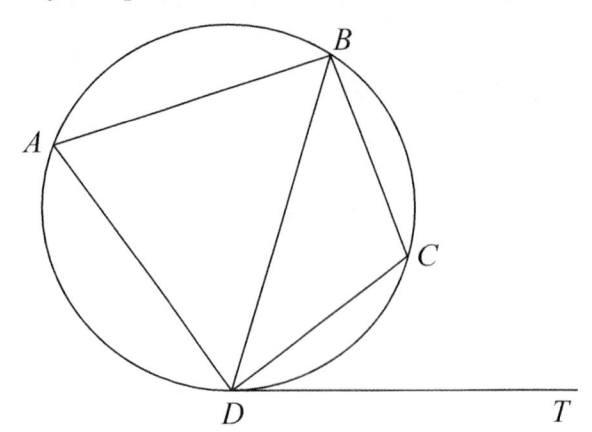

Prove that triangle *BCD* is isosceles.

Answer.................................... (3 marks)

18   The histogram shows information about the marks, in percentage, that some students took maths challenge.

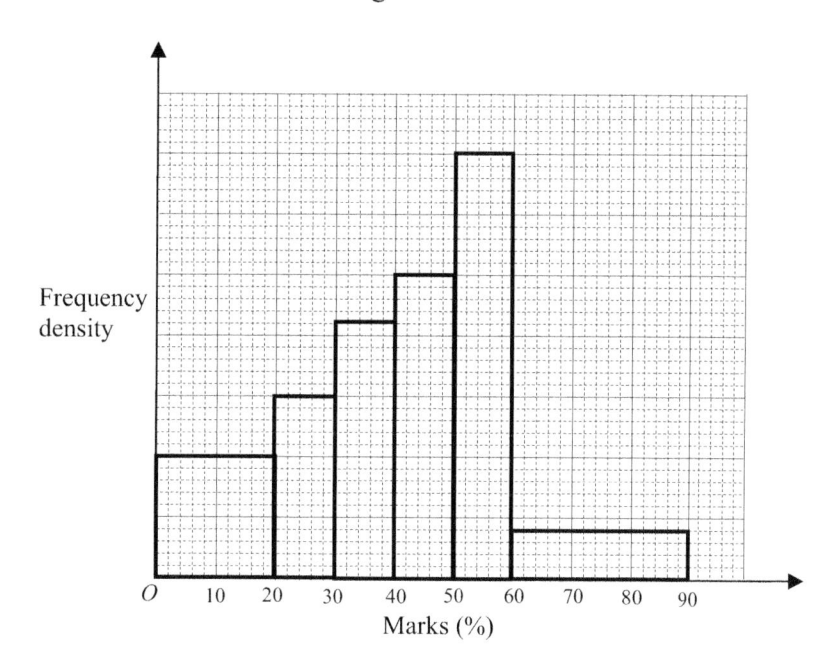

20 students have the marks of less than 20%.

Work out the total number of students.

....
....
....
....
....
....
....
....
....
....

Answer.................................   (5 marks)

19   Jack has 5 black pens, 2 blue pens and 3 red pens in his school bag. He takes two pens from his bag at random.

19(a)   What is the probability that both pens are red?

....

Answer................................ (3 marks)

19(b)   What is the probability that just one pen is red?

....

Answer................................ (3 marks)

20 There are 100 students in Year 10.

All students study at least one of art, drama and music.

8 of the students study art and drama and music.

24 of the students study art and drama.

36 of the students study art and music.

13 of the students study drama and music.

68 of the students study art.

55 of the students study music.

20(a) Draw a Venn diagram to show this information.

....

Answer................................ (3 marks)

20(b) One of the 100 students is selected at random. Find the probability that this student studies drama but not art.

....

Answer................................ (3 marks)

21 OABC is a parallelogram. BCD is a straight line. BD = 3BC. M is the midpoint of OC.

$\vec{OA} = \mathbf{x}$, $\vec{AB} = \mathbf{y}$.

Show by a vector method that AM is parallel to OD.

Answer.................................. (3 marks)

22 Line L has gradient 2 and passes through (2,1).

Work out the equation of the line.

Give your answer in the form $y = mx + c$.

Answer.................................. (2 marks)

23 The curve with equation $y = 4x^2 + \dfrac{1}{x}$ has one stationary point.

Find the coordinates of this stationary point.
Show your working clearly.

Answer……………………….   (2 marks)

24   Here is the graph of $y = 2(x-2)^2 - 1$ for values of x from 0 to 4.

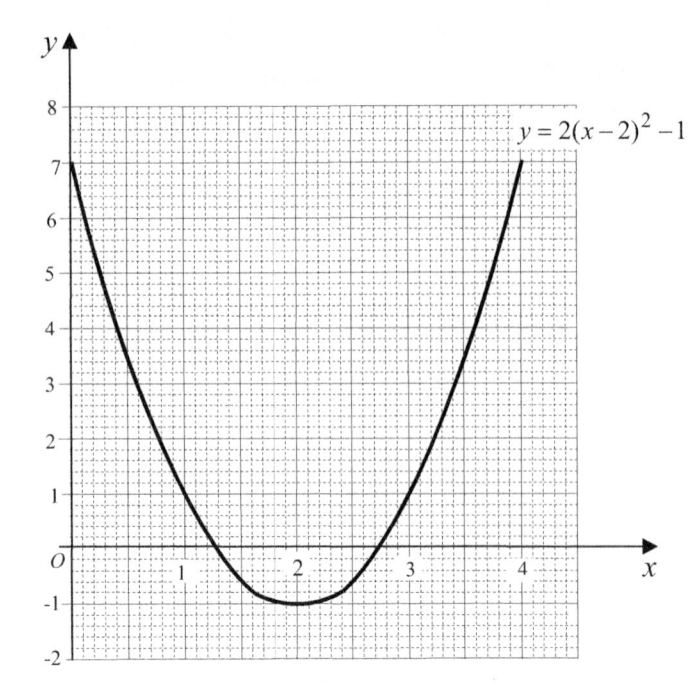

24(a)   Use the Use the graph to find estimates for the solutions of $2(x-2)^2 - 1 = 0$.

Give your answers to 1 decimal place.

Answer……………………………… (2 marks)

24(b)   Use the graph to find estimates for the solutions of the simultaneous equations

(i) $y = 2(x-2)^2 - 1$.

(ii) $y = 2x - 2$

Answer……………………………… (2 marks)

24(c) By drawing a suitable linear graph on the grid, work out approximate solutions of $2x^2 - 9x + 8 = 0$.

Give your answers to 1 decimal place.

....

Answer................................ (4 marks)

25 The diagram shows the graph of $y = \sin x$ for $0° \leq x \leq 360°$

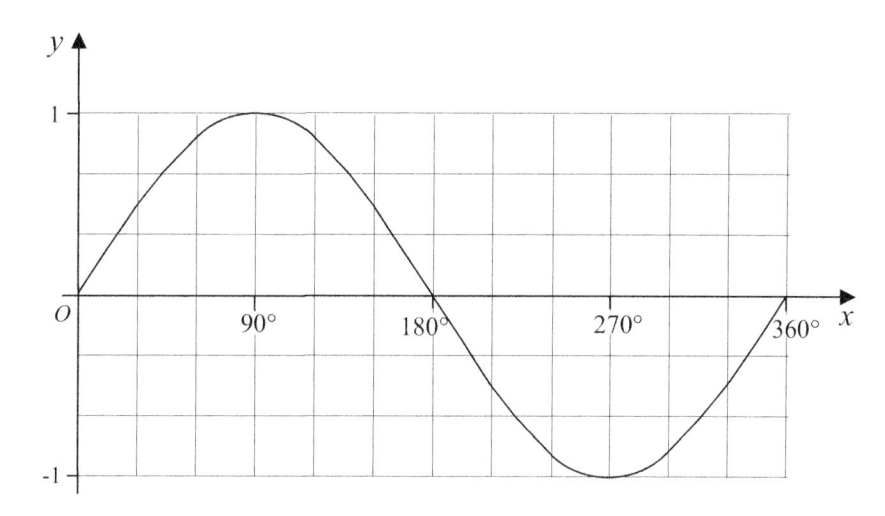

25(a) On the grid above, sketch the graph of $y = \sin(x + 30°)$ for $0° \leq x \leq 360°$

....

(3 marks)

25(b) The graph of $y = \sin(x+30°)+2$ has a minimum at point A for $0° \leq x \leq 360°$. Write down the coordinates of A.

....

....

....

....

....

Answer............................ (3 marks)

Paper 3

Materials

For this paper you must have:
- Ruler graduated in centimetres and millimetres, protractor, compasses, pen, HB pencil, eraser, calculator.
- Tracing paper may be used.

Time allowed

2 hours.

Instructions

- Use black ink or black ball-point pen. Draw diagrams in pencil.
- Answer all questions.
- You must answer the questions in the space provided. Do not write outside the box around each page or on blank pages.
- Do all rough work in this book. Cross through any work that you do not want to be marked.
- In all calculations, show clearly how you work out your answer.

Information

- The marks for questions are shown in brackets.
- The maximum mark is 100.

Advice

- Read each question carefully before you start to answer it.
- Check your answers if you have time at the end.

1 Simplify $p^3 \times p^6$

   Answer……………………………… (3 marks)

2 Simplify fully $\dfrac{9x}{(x+2)(x-4)} - \dfrac{3}{x+2}$

   Answer……………………………… (3 marks)

3 Write down the value of m^0, where $m \neq 0$

   Answer……………………………… (3 marks)

4 Write as a single power of x

   $\left(\dfrac{x^{\frac{4}{3}} \times x^{\frac{5}{3}}}{x} \right)^3$

   Answer……………………………… (3 marks)

5 Factorise fully $(x^2 - 16) - (x+4)^2 + (x+4)(x+1)$

   Answer……………………………… (3 marks)

6 Solve $(1-\sqrt{x})^{\frac{1}{3}} = -2$

   ....
   ....
   ....

   Answer................................. (3 marks)

7 $x^2 + 4x - 5 \equiv (x+a)^2 + b$

   Work out the values of a and b.

   ....
   ....
   ....

   Answer................................. (3 marks)

8 $x : y = 3 : 2$ and $a : b = 5x : 3y$

   Work out $a : b$

   Give your answer in its simplest form.

   ....
   ....
   ....

   Answer................................. (3 marks)

9 Rearrange $p = \dfrac{y}{y-2}$ to make y the subject.

   ....
   ....
   ....

   Answer................................. (3 marks)

10 a is a positive integer, show that $\sqrt{2a}(\sqrt{8a} + a\sqrt{2a})$ is always a multiple of 2.

   ....
   ....
   ....

   (2 marks)

11 The function $f(x)$ is defined as $f(x) = \sqrt{x^2 - 36}$.

State the range of values of x which must be excluded from the domain of $f(x)$

....

....

....

Answer.............................. (3 marks)

12 Solve $3x^2 + 2x - 6 = 0$

Give your solutions to 3 significant figures.

....

....

....

Answer.............................. (3 marks)

13 A clothes shop has a sale.

In the sale, normal prices are reduced by 15%.

13(a) The normal price of a tie is £12.

Work out the sale price of the tie.

....

....

....

Answer.............................. (3 marks)

13(b) The price of a jumper is reduced by £6.00 in the sale.

Work out the normal price of the jumper.

....

....

....

Answer.............................. (2 marks)

14 $y = x^3 - 3x^2 - 9x + 5$

14(a) Find $\frac{dy}{dx}$

Answer.............................. (2 marks)

14(b) The curve with equation $y = x^3 - 3x^2 - 9x + 5$ has two turning points.

Work out the coordinates of these two turning points.

Show your working clearly.

Answer.............................. (4 marks)

15   ξ is a universal set.

ξ = {1,2,3,4,5,6,7,8,9,10,11,12,13,14,15}

A = {3,4,5,8,13,15}

B = {4,6,8,9,11,12}

C = {2,3,4,7,9,11,13}

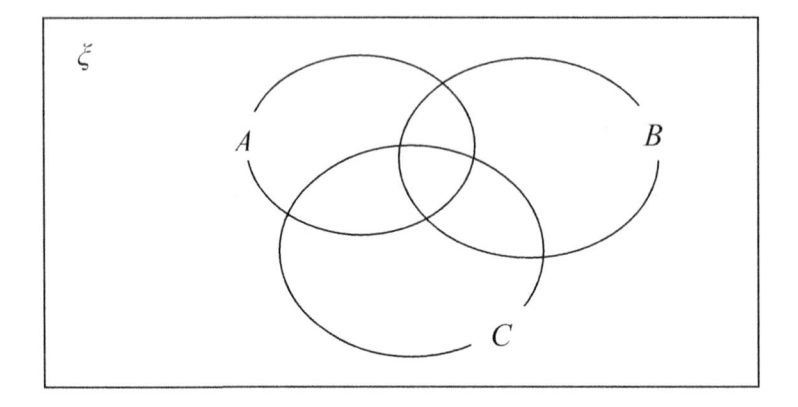

15(a) Complete the Venn diagram.

(4 marks)

15 (b) List the members of the set $(A \cup B)' \cap C$

....

....

....

....

Answer................................   (2 marks)

16   A sphere and a cone have the same volume. The base of the cone and the sphere have the same radius r cm.

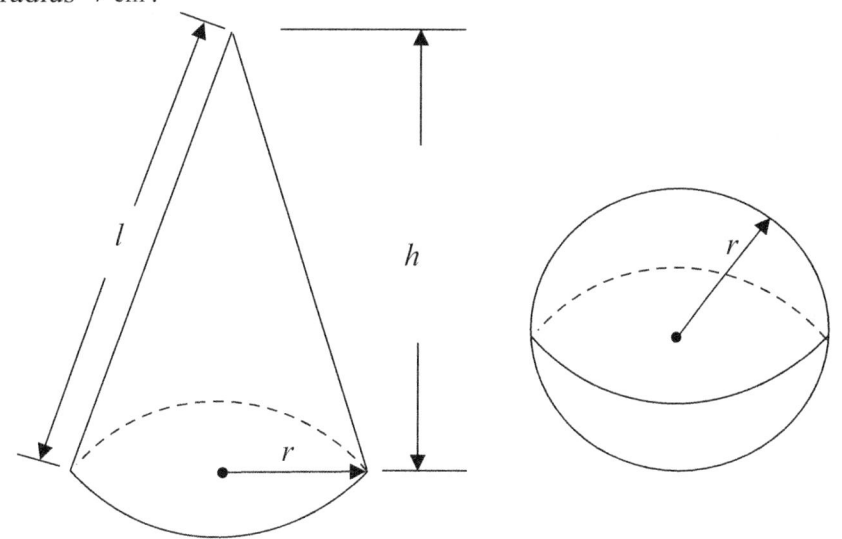

Work out the curved surface area of cone in terms of r.

Answer.................................. (4 marks)

17   QPRS is a cyclic quadrilateral. C is the centre of the circle. ∠QCM = ∠SMR = 80°.

Work out the value of ∠QPR

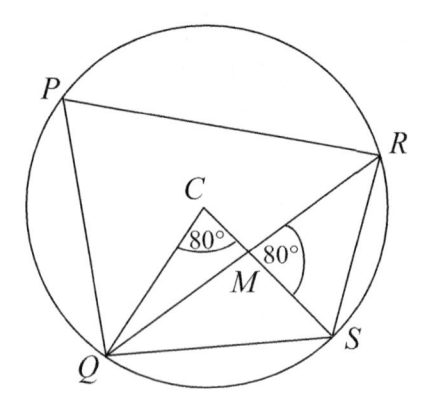

....

....

....

....

....

....

....

....

Answer.................................   (4 marks)

18   Here are a trapezium and a right-angled triangle.

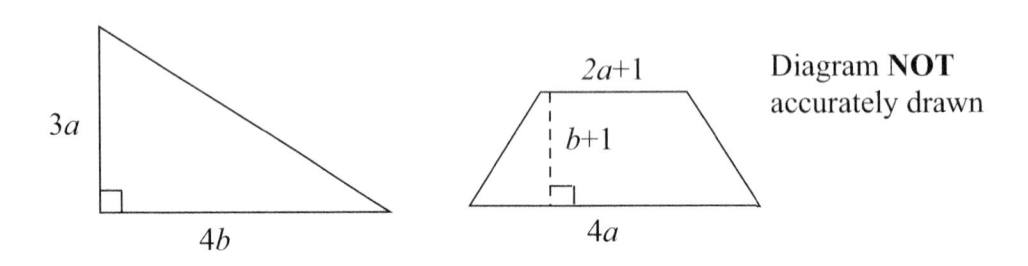

Diagram **NOT** accurately drawn

The area of the triangle is equal to the area of trapezium.

Find an expression for a in terms of b, where $b>1$

....

....

....

....

Answer.................................   (4 marks)

19   Here is a list of members written in order of size.

   3   6   x   12   y   16

   The numbers have a median of 11 and have a mean of 10.

   Find the values of x and y.

   Answer................................   (2 marks)

20   A box contains toy cars. Each car is red or black or blue or silver.

   Jack takes a car at random from the box.

   The table shows the probabilities that Jack takes a red car or a blue car or a black car or silver.

Colour of car	Probability
red	0.50
blue	0.30
black	0.075
silver	

20(a)   Work out the probability that Jack takes a silver car.

   Answer................................   (2 marks)

20(b) Jack adds 50 black cars into the box. The following table shows the probabilities that Jack takes a red car or a blue car or a black car or silver after he adds 50 black cars into the box.

Colour of car	Probability
red	0.40
blue	0.24
black	0.26
silver	0.10

Work out the total number of cars in the box originally.

....

....

....

....

Answer................................ (4 marks)

21 Line L passes through (6,1) and (3,3).

Work out the equation of the line.

Give your answer in the form $ax + by = c$, where a, b and c are integers.

....

....

....

....

Answer................................ (2 marks)

22 The graph shows two lines. L2 is a of L1: $y = 2 - 2x$ through $x = 1$.

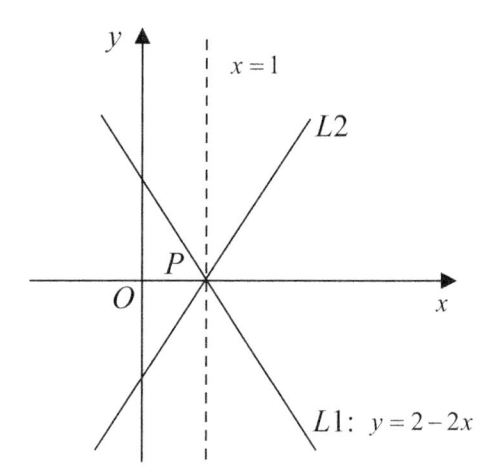

Work out the equation of L2.

Give your answer in the form $y = mx + c$.

Answer.............................. (2 marks)

23 The diagram shows a circle, centre *C*. *TP* is a tangent to the circle and intersects the *x*-axis at *T*.

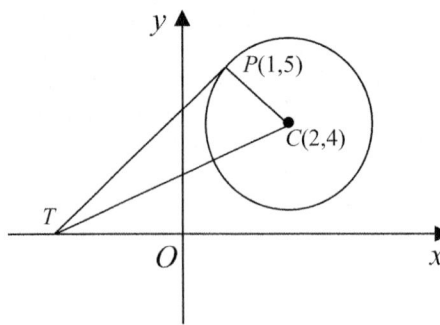

Work out the length of *TP*

Answer.............................. (3 marks)

24(a) Describe fully the single transformation that maps shape **P** onto shape **Q**.

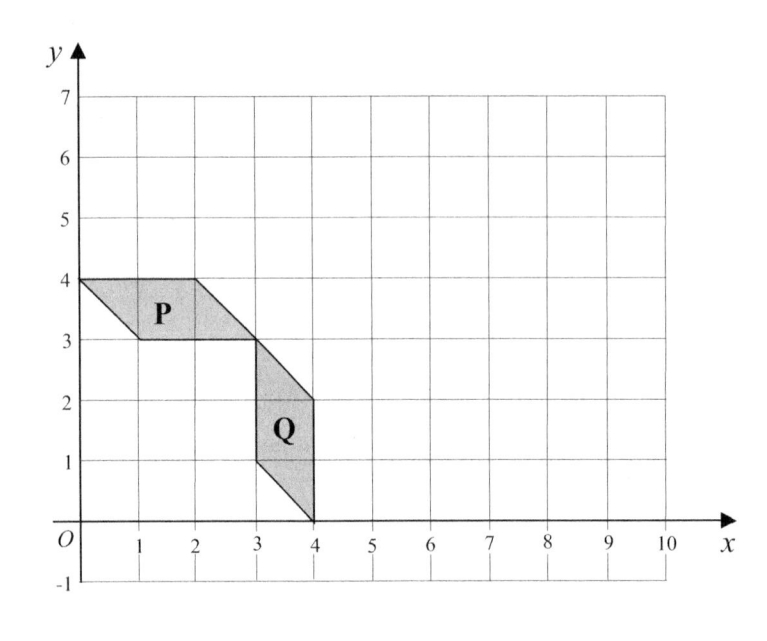

Answer.............................. (2 marks)

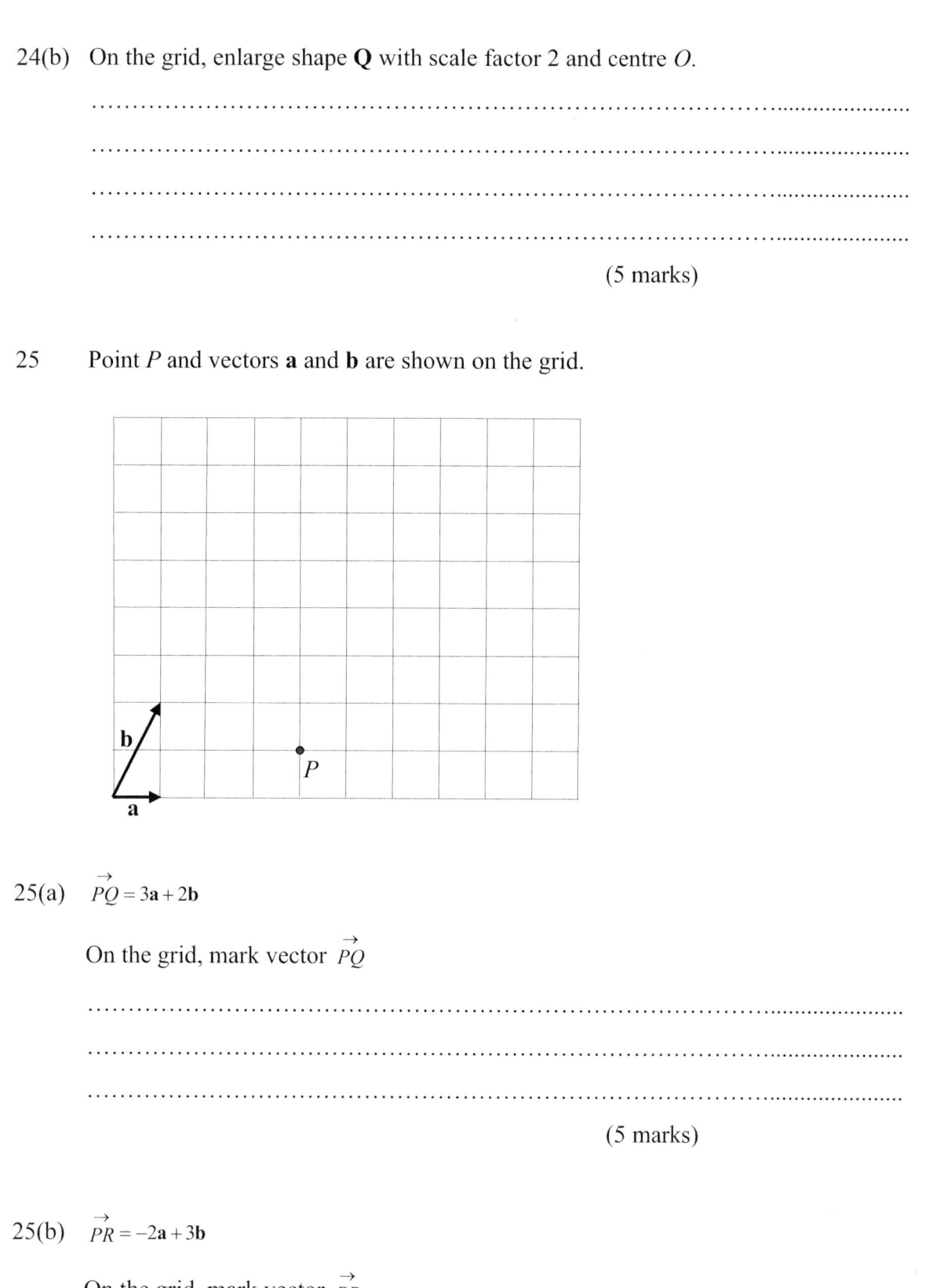

24(b) On the grid, enlarge shape **Q** with scale factor 2 and centre *O*.

....
....
....
....

(5 marks)

25   Point *P* and vectors **a** and **b** are shown on the grid.

25(a) $\vec{PQ} = 3\mathbf{a} + 2\mathbf{b}$

On the grid, mark vector $\vec{PQ}$

....
....
....

(5 marks)

25(b) $\vec{PR} = -2\mathbf{a} + 3\mathbf{b}$

On the grid, mark vector $\vec{PR}$

....
....
....

(5 marks)

25(c) Find vector $\vec{QR}$, in terms of **a** and **b**.

....

....

....

....

Answer……………………………… (4 marks)

Paper 4

Materials

For this paper you must have:
- Ruler graduated in centimetres and millimetres, protractor, compasses, pen, HB pencil, eraser, calculator.
- Tracing paper may be used.

Time allowed

2 hours.

Instructions
- Use black ink or black ball-point pen. Draw diagrams in pencil.
- Answer all questions.
- You must answer the questions in the space provided. Do not write outside the box around each page or on blank pages.
- Do all rough work in this book. Cross through any work that you do not want to be marked.
- In all calculations, show clearly how you work out your answer.

Information
- The marks for questions are shown in brackets.
- The maximum mark is 100.

Advice
- Read each question carefully before you start to answer it.
- Check your answers if you have time at the end.

1   Expand and Simplify $(x-2)(x-1)(x+1)$

    Answer…………………………….   (2 marks)

2   Factorise fully $9x^4 - 36x^2$.

    Answer…………………………….   (2 marks)

3   Simplify $\dfrac{x^2 + 4x + 4}{x^2 - 2x - 8}$

    Answer…………………………….   (3 marks)

4   60% of p = 30% of q.

    Work out p as a percentage of q.

    Answer…………………………….   (3 marks)

5   $x : y = 2 : 3$ and z is 30% of y.

    Work out $x : z$

    Answer…………………………….   (3 marks)

6 The function $f(x)$ is defined as $f(x) = \dfrac{1}{x^2+8x+15}$.

State the values of x which must be excluded from the domain of $f(x)$

Answer……………………….…. (2 marks)

7 $f(x) = 2\cos x - 2$ for $0° \leq x \leq 360°$

Work out the range of $f(x)$.

Answer……………………….…. (3 marks)

8 $g(x) = x^2 - 4$

The range of $g(x)$ is $g(x) \leq 5$

Work out the domain of $g(x)$.

Answer……………………….…. (3 marks)

9 $f(n) = n^2$ for all positive integer values of n.

Prove that $f(n+1) - f(n)$ is always odd.

Answer……………………….…. (3 marks)

10 There are 20 boys and 10 girls in a class. They took maths challenge. The mean mark that the boys have is 65%, while the mean mark that the girls have is 62%. Work out the mean mark that the 30 children have.

Answer……………………….   (3 marks)

11 The 10th term of an arithmetic series, S, is 20. The sum of the first 10 terms of S is 290.
Find the 5th term of S.
Show your working clearly.

Answer……………………….   (3 marks)

12 On 1 April 2018, the cost of 5 grams of gold was £200. The cost of gold increased by 2.5% from 1 April 2018 to 1 April 2019.
Work out the cost of 20 grams of gold on 1 April 2019.

Answer……………………….   (3 marks)

13 Show that $3\frac{2}{5} \div 1\frac{9}{25} = 2\frac{1}{2}$

....

....

....

....

(3 marks)

14 Rationalise the denominator and simply fully $\frac{\sqrt{3}-1}{2-\sqrt{3}}$

....

....

....

....

Answer................................ (3 marks)

15 A car travels a distance of 62.5 km, correct to the nearest 0.5 km. The car takes

45.8 minutes correct to 1 decimal place.

Work out the lower bound for the average speed of the car.

Show your working clearly.

Give your answer in km/h correct to 1 decimal place.

....

....

....

....

....

....

....

Answer................................ (3 marks)

16   The diagram shows a trapezium

Work out the value of x

Give your answer to 1 decimal place.

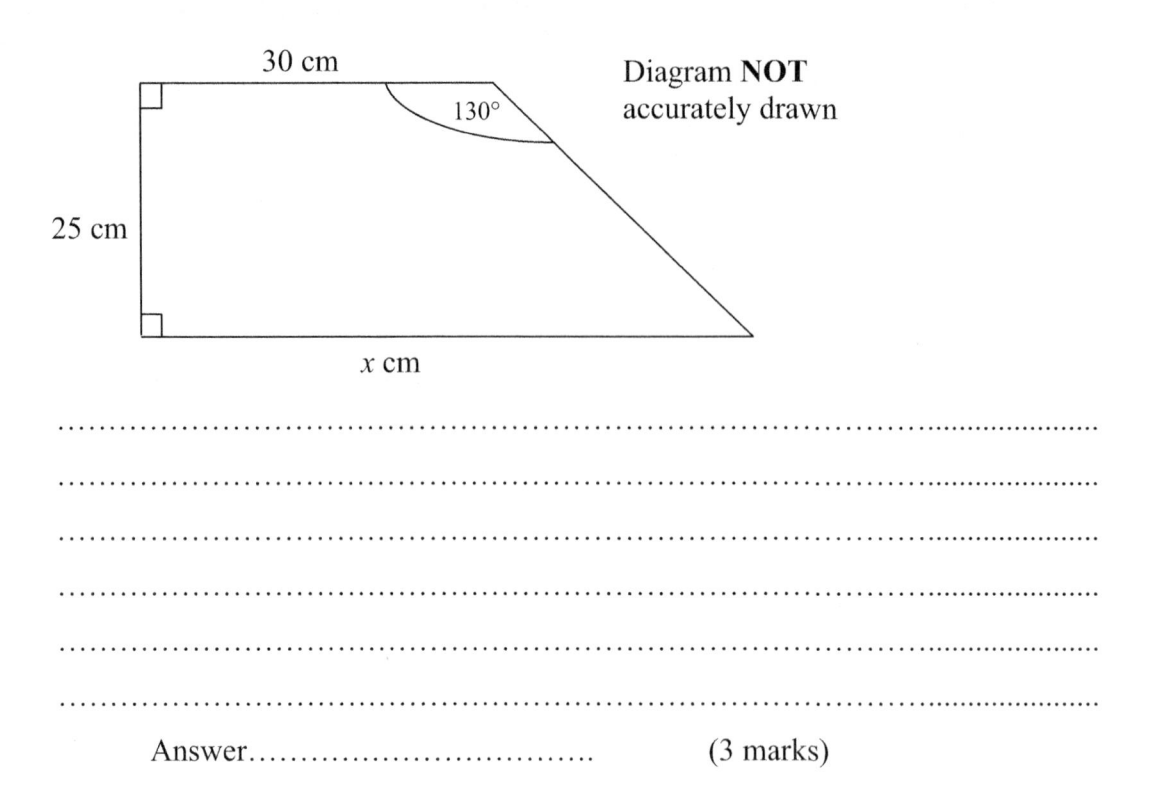

30 cm

130°

25 cm

x cm

Diagram **NOT** accurately drawn

Answer................................ (3 marks)

17   A circle touches all vertices of the square. The radius of the circle is 5 cm as shown.

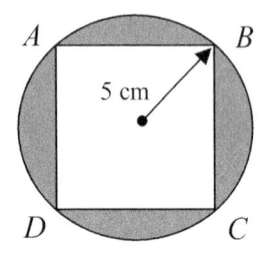

5 cm

A   B

D   C

Work out the total shaded area.

Give your answer to 2 decimal places.

Answer................................ (3 marks)

18 ABCD is a cyclic quadrilateral. O is the centre of the circle.

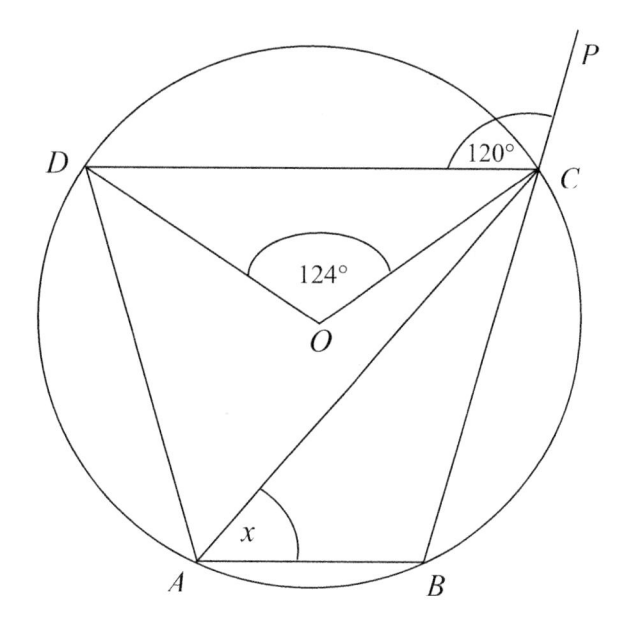

Work out the value of x.

....

Answer.............................. (4 marks)

19 The diagram shows a solid prism. The top *EFGH* is a rectangle of width 20 cm and length 30 cm, the base *ABCD* is rectangle of width 20 cm and length 50 cm. The line joining the centres of the top and the base is perpendicular to both and is 40 cm long. The prism is made from wood with density 0.0007 kg/cm³.

Work out the mass of the prism.

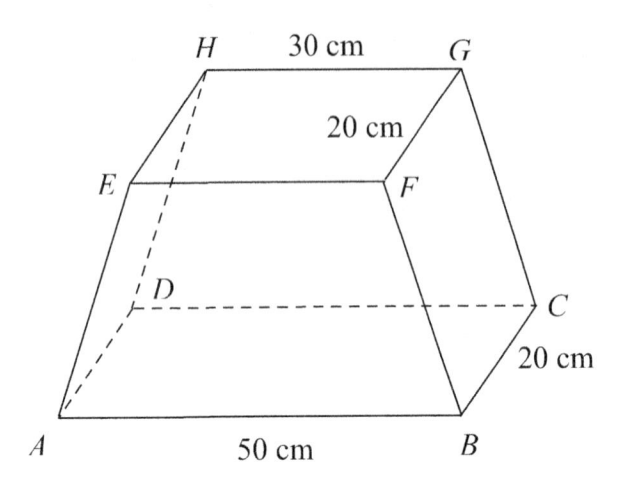

Answer.................................. (4 marks)

20 The table shows information about the amount of money that 100 people spent in a shop.

Amount of money (£)	Frequency
$0 < m \leq 10$	6
$10 < m \leq 20$	15
$20 < m \leq 30$	22
$30 < m \leq 40$	35
$40 < m \leq 50$	16
$50 < m \leq 60$	6

20(a) Complete the cumulative frequency table

Amount of money (£)	Cumulative Frequency
$0 < m \leq 10$	
$0 < m \leq 20$	
$0 < m \leq 30$	
$0 < m \leq 40$	
$0 < m \leq 50$	
$0 < m \leq 60$	

(6 marks)

20(b) On the grid, draw a cumulative frequency graph for your table.

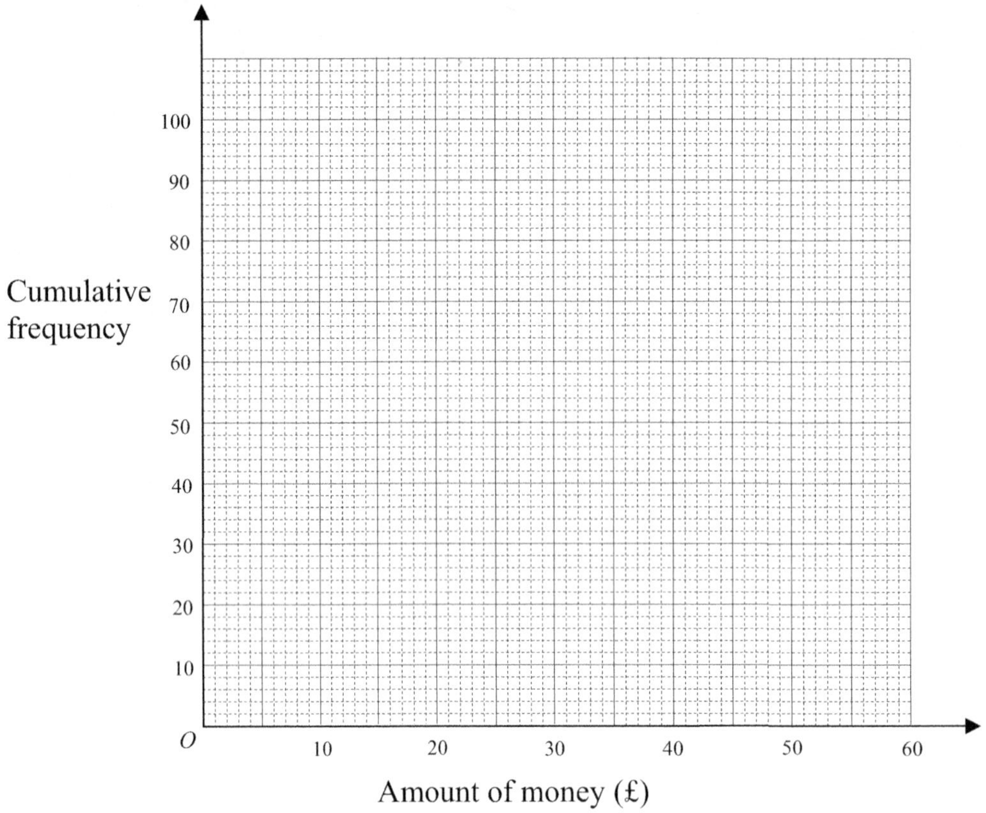

(6 marks)

20(c) Use your graph to complete the table below.

Give your answer to the nearest pound.

Lower quartile (£)	
Median (£)	
Upper quartile (£)	
Interquartile range (£)	

(4 marks)

10

21   Jack has 5 black beads, 2 blue beads and 3 red beads in a bag. He takes a bead at random from the bag and put it back. Then he takes the second bead at random from the bag.

21 (a)   What is the probability that both beads are red?

....

Answer................................   (4 marks)

21(b)   What is the probability that just one bead is red?

Answer................................   (3 marks)

22   Line *L* passes through (2,1) and (3,3).

Work out the equation of the line.

Give your answer in the form $y = mx + c$.

Answer................................   (2 marks)

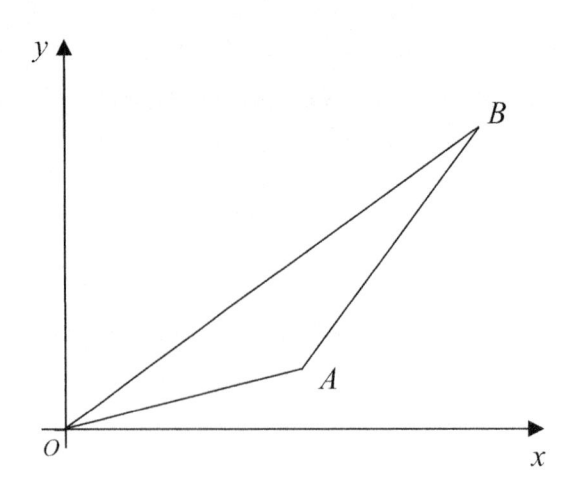

23   OAB is a triangle.

$\vec{OA} = \begin{pmatrix} 4 \\ 1 \end{pmatrix}$, $\vec{OB} = \begin{pmatrix} 7 \\ 5 \end{pmatrix}$

Work out the magnitude of $\vec{AB}$

....
....
....
....

Answer................................   (3 marks)

24   The diagram shows the graph of $y = \cos x$ for $0° \leq x \leq 360°$

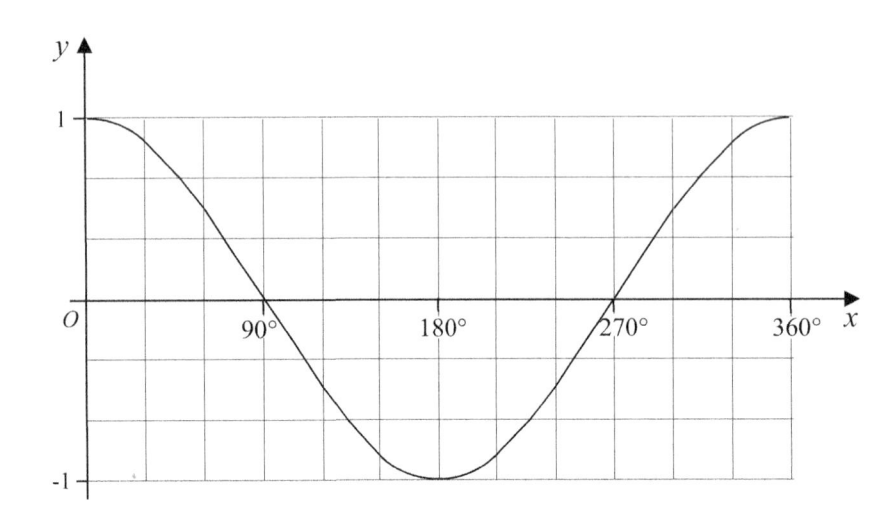

24(a)   On the grid above, sketch the graph of $y = \cos(x + 60°)$ for $0° \leq x \leq 360°$

....

(3 marks)

24(b) The graph of $y = 2\cos(x+60°)+1$ has a maximum at point A for $0° \leq x \leq 360°$. Write down the coordinates of A.

....

....

....

Answer............................. (3 marks)

25 ξ is a universal set.

$n(\xi) = 35, n(A) = 8, n(B) = 10, n(C) = 14, n(B \cap C) = 4, n(A \cap C) = 3$.

25(a) Complete the Venn diagram to show the number of elements in each region of the Venn diagram.

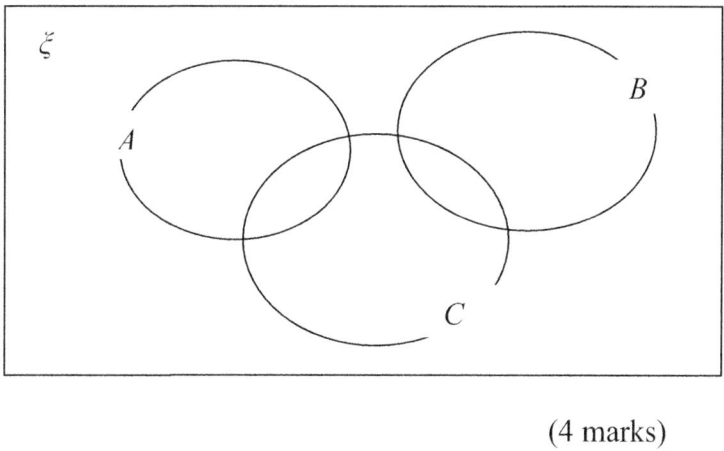

(4 marks)

25(b) Find $n(A \cup C)$

....

....

....

Answer............................. (3 marks)

25(c) Find $n(C \cap B')$

....

....

....

Answer............................. (3 marks)

Paper 1 solutions

1. Find the lowest common multiple (LCM) of 10, 30 and 45

    $10 = 2 \times 5$, $30 = 2 \times 3 \times 5$, $45 = 3 \times 3 \times 5$

    $\therefore$ LCM $= 2 \times 3 \times 3 \times 5 = 90$

    Answer 90 (2 marks)

2. Find the highest common factor (HCF) of 15, 30 and 45

    $15 = 3 \times 5$, $30 = 2 \times 3 \times 5$, $45 = 3 \times 3 \times 5$

    $\therefore$ HCF $= 3 \times 5 = 15$

    Answer 15 (2 marks)

3. The first four terms of an arithmetic sequence are

     5 11 17 23

    Work out an expression, in terms of n, for the nth term.

    $a_n = a_1 + (n-1)d$

    $\Rightarrow a_2 = a_1 + d \Rightarrow d = a_2 - a_1 \Rightarrow d = 11 - 5 = 6$, where $n = 2$.

    $\therefore\ a_n = 5 + 6(n-1) = 6n - 1$

    Answer $6n - 1$ (2 marks)

4. Jack, Mark and Sam share some money in the ratio 3:4:5. Sam gets £15 more than Mark.

    Work out the amount of money that Jack gets.

    Sam gets £15 more than Mark, if the sum of the money is a, then

    $\dfrac{5}{12}a - \dfrac{4}{12}a = 15 \Rightarrow a = 12 \times 15$

    The amount of money that Jack gets $= \dfrac{3}{12}a = \dfrac{3}{12} \times 12 \times 15 = 45$

    Answer £45 (2 marks)

5   Use algebra to show that the recurring decimal $0.\dot{2}0\dot{7} = \frac{23}{111}$

$x = 0.\dot{2}0\dot{7}$ (1)

$1000x = 207.\dot{2}0\dot{7}$ (2)

Eq. (2)-Eq. (1) $\Rightarrow 999x = 207 \Rightarrow x = \frac{207}{999} = \frac{23}{111}$

$\therefore 0.\dot{2}0\dot{7} = \frac{23}{111}$ (3 marks)

6(a) Write 1.3×10^{-3} as an ordinary number.

     Answer   0.0013   (1 mark)

6(b) Here are three numbers written in standard form.

Arrange these numbers in order of size.

Start with the smallest number.

3.4×10^{-7} 5.5×10^{-8} 2.1×10^{-6}

     Answer 5.5×10^{-8} 3.4×10^{-7} 2.1×10^{-6}

     (2 marks)

7 $\begin{pmatrix} 3+y & -3 \\ 2 & 1 \end{pmatrix} \begin{pmatrix} -2 \\ x \end{pmatrix} = \begin{pmatrix} -8 \\ 2 \end{pmatrix}$

Find the value of x and the value of y.

$\begin{pmatrix} 3+y & -3 \\ 2 & 1 \end{pmatrix} \begin{pmatrix} -2 \\ x \end{pmatrix} = \begin{pmatrix} -8 \\ 2 \end{pmatrix} \Rightarrow \begin{pmatrix} -6-2y-3x \\ -4+x \end{pmatrix} = \begin{pmatrix} -8 \\ 2 \end{pmatrix} \Rightarrow x = 6, y = \frac{8-6-3x}{2} = -8$

     Answer $x = 6, y = -8$ (2 marks)

8   In Hong Kong, Alice bought 4 boxes of chocolate, each costing 52 HKD (Hong Kong Dollars). Alice also bought 2 watches, each costing 450 HKD.

The exchange rate was £1=11.85 HKD.

Calculate the total cost of these six items, in £, to the nearest pound.

$\frac{4 \times 52 + 2 \times 450}{11.85} = 93.5$

$\therefore$ The total cost of these six items is £94

     Answer   £94   (3 marks)

9 Without using a calculator, evaluate $\dfrac{\sqrt{72}-\sqrt{32}}{\sqrt{50}}$

$$\dfrac{\sqrt{72}-\sqrt{32}}{\sqrt{50}} = \dfrac{6\sqrt{2}-4\sqrt{2}}{5\sqrt{2}} = \dfrac{2}{5} = 0.4$$

Answer 0.4 (2 marks)

10 a, b, c and d are four integers.

Their mean is 9.5, their mode is 8, and their median is 9.

10(a) Find the value of the largest of the four integers.

Their median is 9 and their mode is $8 \Rightarrow b=8, c=10$ and $a=8$

Their mean is $9.5 \Rightarrow d = 4 \times 9.5 - a - b - c = 4 \times 9.5 - 8 - 8 - 10 = 12$

Answer 12 (3 marks)

10(b) Find the mean value of the numbers $(3a-4)$, $(3b-4)$, $(3c-4)$ and $(3d-4)$.

The mean value of the numbers is:

$$\dfrac{3a-4+3b-4+3c-4+3d-4}{4} = \dfrac{3(a+b+c+d)}{4} - 4 = 3 \times 9.5 - 4 = 24.5$$

Answer 24.5 (2 marks)

11(a) Write $2x^2 - 8x + 5$ in the form $a(x+b)^2 + c$

$2x^2 - 8x + 5 = 2(x-2)^2 - 8 + 5 = 2(x-2)^2 - 3$

Answer $2(x-2)^2 - 3$ (3 marks)

11(b) Line L is the line of symmetry of the curve with equation $y = 2x^2 - 8x + 5$

Using your answer to part (a) or otherwise, work out the equation of L.

From part (a), $y = 2x^2 - 8x + 5 = 2(x-2)^2 - 3$

∴ The equation of L is $x = 2$

Answer $x = 2$ (3 marks)

12   P is inversely proportional to Q^2 where $Q > 0$. $P = 100$ when $Q = 6$.

Find the value of Q when $P = 16$.

$P = \dfrac{k}{Q^2} \Rightarrow 100 = \dfrac{k}{6^2} \Rightarrow k = 3600$

$\because Q > 0,\ Q = \sqrt{\dfrac{k}{P}} = \sqrt{\dfrac{3600}{16}} = \dfrac{60}{4} = 15$

Answer   15   (3 marks)

13   $A = \{2, 3, 4, 6, 8, 10, 12, 14\}$, $B = \{3, 6, 9, 10\}$. List the members of the set.

13(a) $A \cup B$

$A \cup B = \{2, 3, 4, 6, 8, 9, 10, 12, 14\}$

Answer $\{2, 3, 4, 6, 8, 9, 10, 12, 14\}$ (3 marks)

13(b) $A \cap B$

$A \cap B = \{3, 6, 10\}$

Answer $\{3, 6, 10\}$ (3 marks)

14   $y = \dfrac{3a}{2b - c}$

$a = 43$ correct to 2 significant figures.

$b = 26$ correct to 2 significant figures.

$c = 32$ correct to 2 significant figures.

Work out the lower bound for the value of y.

Give your answer correct to 2 significant figures.

Show your working clearly.

$42.5 \leq a < 43.5$, $25.5 \leq b < 26.5$, $31.5 \leq c < 32.5$

The lower bound for the value of $y = \dfrac{3 \times 42.5}{2 \times 26.5 - 31.5} = 5.9$

Answer   5.9   (4 marks)

15 *ABC* is a right-angled triangle. $\angle B = 90°$, $\angle A = 40°$, $AC = 18$ cm. Calculate the length of *BC*.

Give your answer to 3 significant figures.

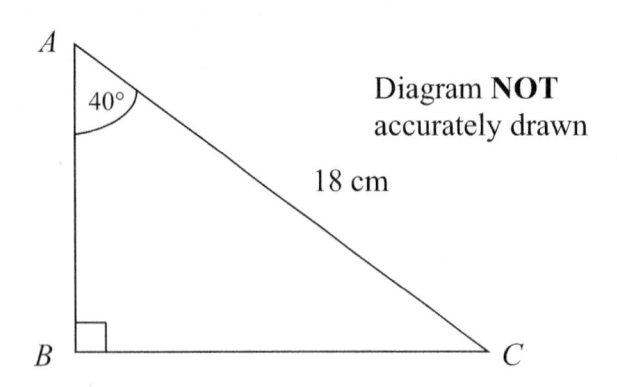

Diagram **NOT** accurately drawn

$BC = AC \times \sin 40° = 18 \sin 40° = 11.6$

Answer   11.6 cm   (3 marks)

16 The regular pentagon *ABCDE* is drawn inside the regular octagon *ABFGHIJK*. They share side *AB*.

Work out the value of *x*.

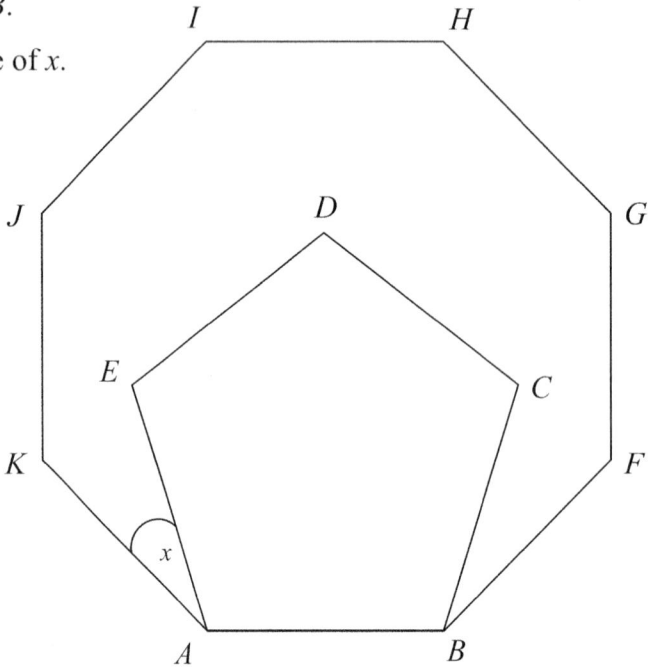

$\angle EAB = \dfrac{(5-2)}{5} \times 180° = 108°$, $\angle KAB = \dfrac{(8-2)}{8} \times 180° = 135°$

$x = \angle KAB - \angle EAB = 135° - 108° = 27°$

Answer   27°   (3 marks)

17 *ABCD* are on the circumference of a circle. *AE* is a tangent to the circle.

Work out ∠*ACD*

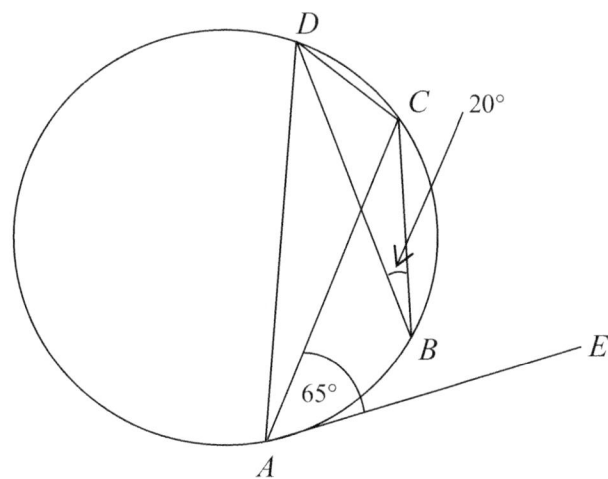

ABCD are on the circumference of a circle, ∴ ∠*CAD* = ∠*CBD* = 20°,

AE is a tangent to the circle, ∴ ∠*CDA* = ∠*CAE* = 65°

In triangle *ACD*, ∠*ACD* = 180° − ∠*CAD* − ∠*CDA* = 180° − 20° − 65° = 95°

Answer   95°   (3 marks)

18 The table shows information about the height of some plants.

Height (cm)	$0 < h \leq 20$	$20 < h \leq 30$	$30 < h \leq 40$	$40 < h \leq 70$
Number of plants	24	38	33	30

The histogram for the height of less than 20 cm of the plants is drawn on the graph.

Complete the histogram for this information.

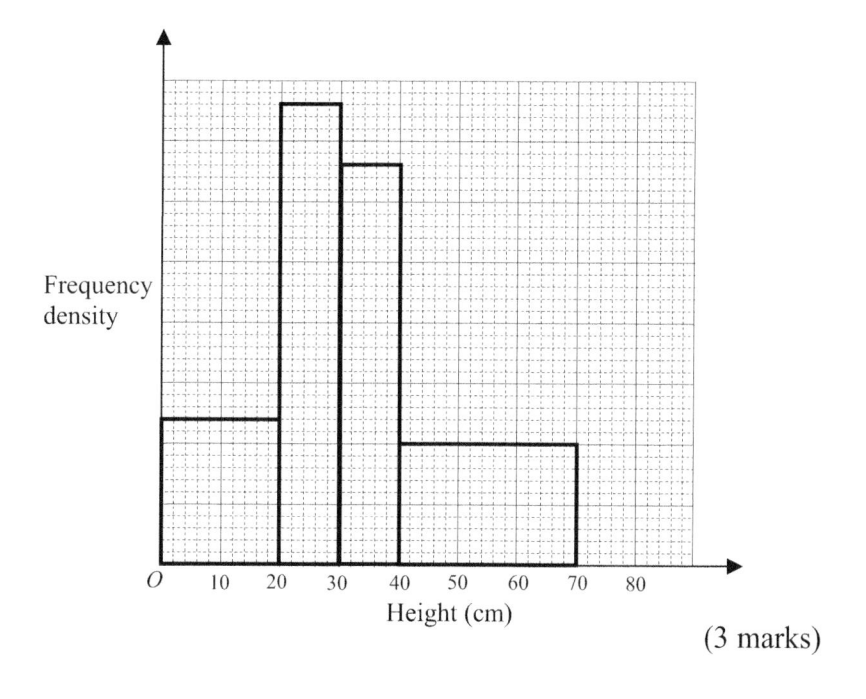

(3 marks)

19   Emma and Jack race against each other in a competition. The probability that Emma wins is 0.6 each time. A draw is not possible. They run two races.

19(a) Complete and fully label the probability tree diagram to show the possible outcome.

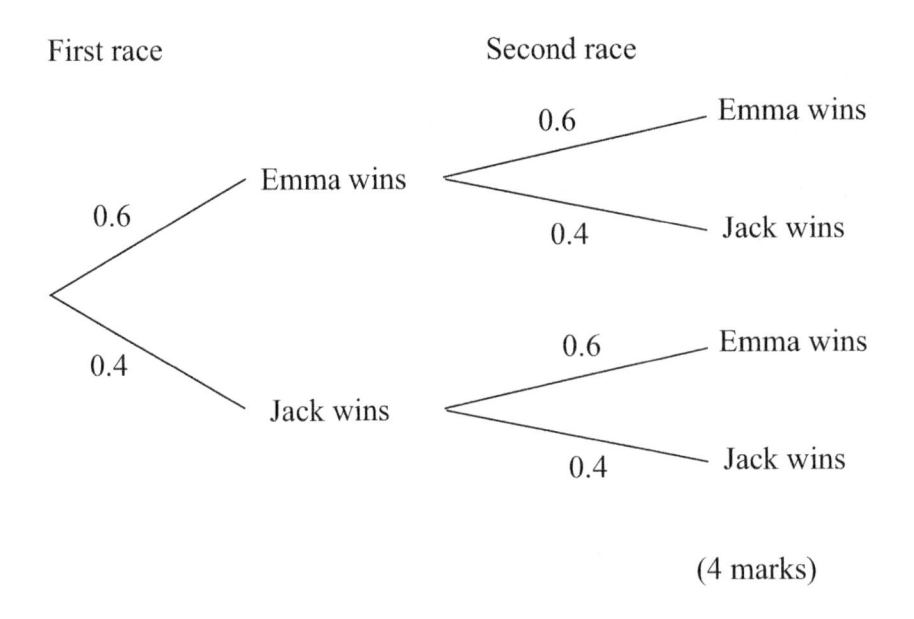

First race   Second race

                         0.6   Emma wins
            Emma wins
  0.6   0.4   Jack wins

                         0.6   Emma wins
  0.4
            Jack wins
                         0.4   Jack wins

(4 marks)

19(b) Calculate the probability that each of them wins only one race.

From the probability tree diagram, the probability that each of them wins only one race is $0.6 \times 0.4 \times 2 = 0.48$

Answer   0.48   (3 marks)

20   The points O, A, B and C are such that
$$\vec{OA} = \begin{pmatrix} 1 \\ 1 \end{pmatrix} \quad \vec{AB} = \begin{pmatrix} 3 \\ 2 \end{pmatrix} \quad \vec{OC} = \begin{pmatrix} 5 \\ 6 \end{pmatrix}$$

Find $\vec{BC}$ as a column vector

$\vec{OC} = \vec{OA} + \vec{AB} + \vec{BC} \Rightarrow \vec{BC} = \vec{OC} - \vec{OA} - \vec{AB} = \begin{pmatrix} 5 \\ 6 \end{pmatrix} - \begin{pmatrix} 1 \\ 1 \end{pmatrix} - \begin{pmatrix} 3 \\ 2 \end{pmatrix} = \begin{pmatrix} 1 \\ 3 \end{pmatrix}$

Answer $\begin{pmatrix} 1 \\ 3 \end{pmatrix}$ (3 marks)

21   *A* is the point with coordinates (-3,2) and *B* is the point with coordinates (13,10).

21(a)   Calculate the gradient of the straight line *AB*.

The gradient of the straight line $AB = \frac{10-2}{13+3} = \frac{1}{2}$

Answer $\frac{1}{2}$ (3 marks)

21(b)   Calculate the length of *AB*.

Give your answer to 1 decimal place.

The length of $AB = \sqrt{(10-2)^2 + (13+3)^2} = 17.9$

Answer   17.9 units   (3 marks)

22   On the grid below indicate clearly the region *R* defined by the three inequalities.

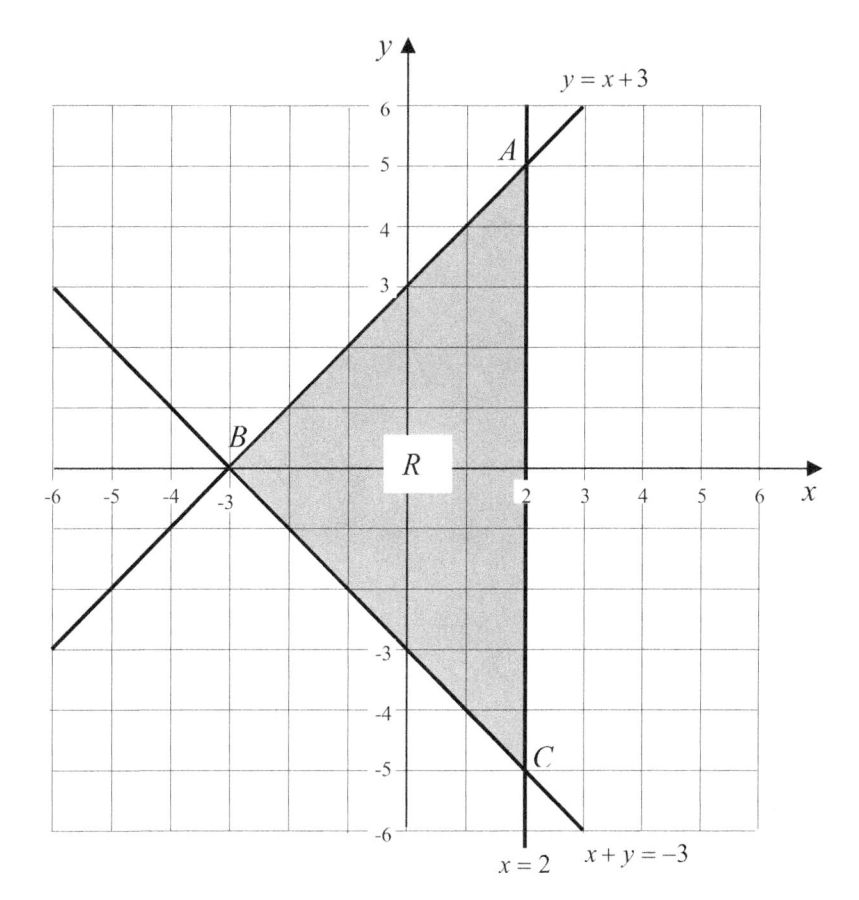

$x \leq 2$

$y \leq x+3$

$y \geq -x-3$

22(a)   Label the region clearly with an *R*.

As shown on the diagram.   (3 marks)

22(b) Calculate the area of the region R.

The area of the region $R = \dfrac{(A_y - C_y)(A_x - B_x)}{2} = \dfrac{(5+5)(2+3)}{2} = 25$

Answer   25 square units.   (3 marks)

23(a) Describe fully the single transformation that maps triangle **P** onto triangle **Q**.

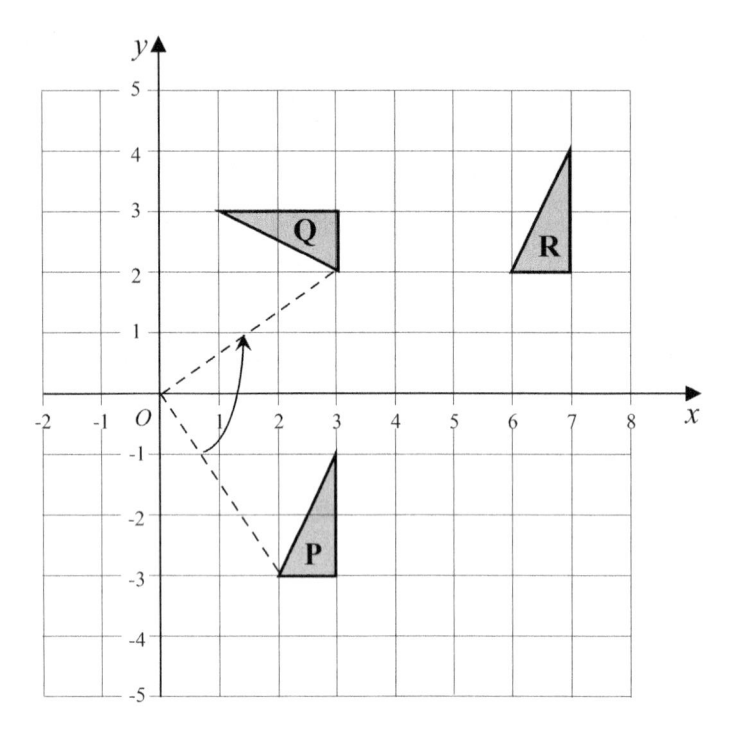

Answer   Rotation by $90°$, centre the origin.

(3 marks)

23(b) On the grid, translate triangle **P** 4 squares to the right and 5 squares up. Label the new triangle **R**.

As shown on the diagram.   (3 marks)

24 The diagram shows the graph of $y = \sin x$ for $0° \le x \le 360°$

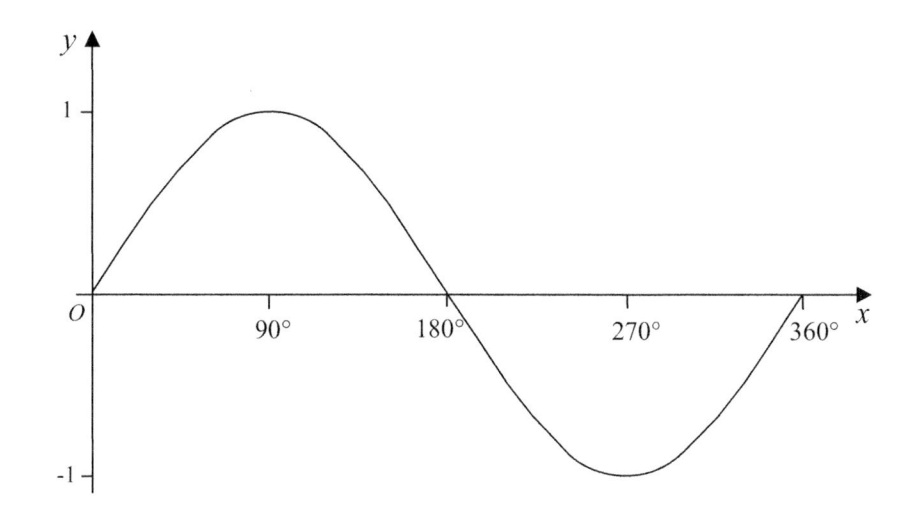

The two diagrams below show the graphs of transformations of $y = \sin x$

Write down the equation of each graph.

24(a)

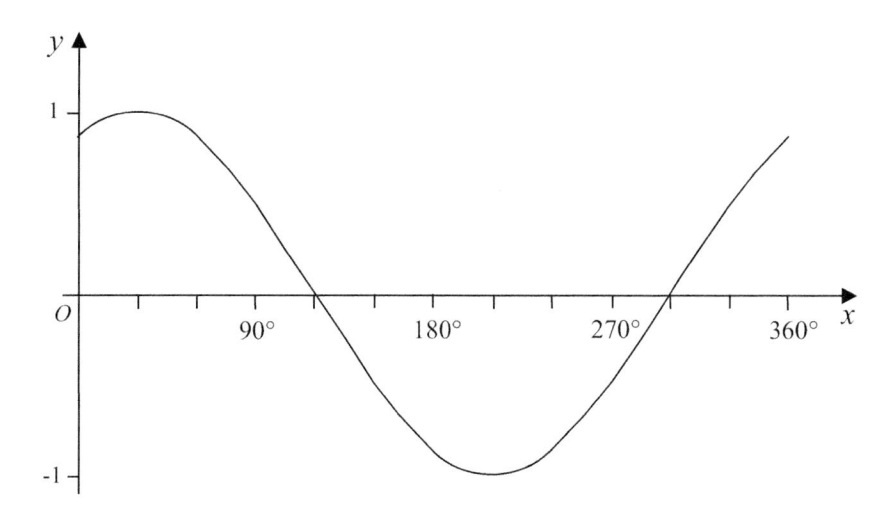

Answer $y = \sin(x + 60°)$ (3 marks)

24(b)

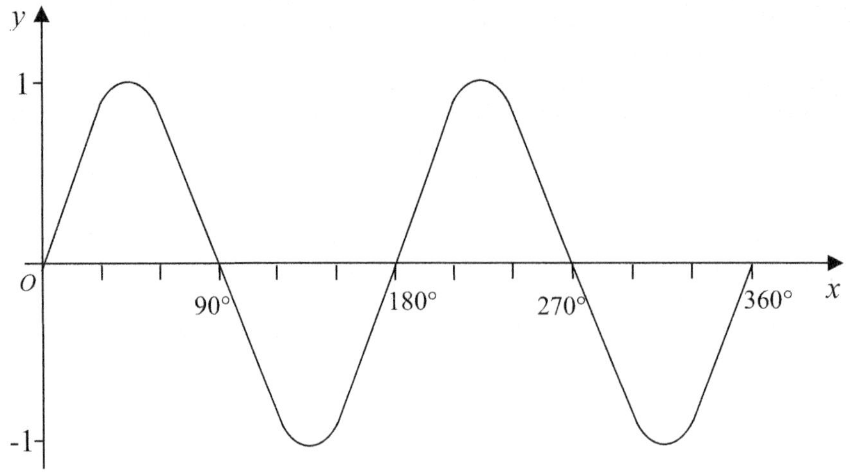

Answer $y = \sin(2x)$ (3 marks)

25 The diagram shows parts of the graph of $y = f(x)$ and $y = g(x)$.

25(a) Find $g(3)$

From the graph, $g(3) = -1$

Answer -1 (3 marks)

25(b) Find $gf(-2)$

From the graph, $f(-2) = -4$, $g(-4) = 0$

$gf(-2) = g(-4) = 0$

$\therefore gf(-2) = 0$

Answer 0 (3 marks)

9

25(c) Calculate an estimate for the gradient of the curve $y = f(x)$ at the point on the curve where $x = -2$.

Draw line L, the tangent to the curve $y = f(x)$ at the point on the curve where $x = -2$

Line L passes through (-2,-4) and (0,-2).

∴ the gradient is $\dfrac{-4+2}{-2-0} = 1$

Answer   1   (3 marks)

Paper 2 solutions

1 Expand $(3+2\sqrt{3})^2$

Give your answer in the form $a+b\sqrt{3}$, where a and b are integers.

Show your working clearly.

$(3+2\sqrt{3})^2 = 3^2 + (2\sqrt{3})^2 + 2\times 3\times 2\sqrt{3} = 9+4\times 3+12\sqrt{3} = 21+12\sqrt{3}$

  Answer $21+12\sqrt{3}$ (2 marks)

2 Simplify the expression $(2x^3 y^2)^4$

$(2x^3 y^2)^4 = 2^4 x^{3\times 4} y^{2\times 4} = 16x^{12} y^8$

  Answer $16x^{12}y^8$ (2 marks)

3 Solve the simultaneous equations

$2x+y=13$

$x-y=8$

$2x+y=13$ (1)

$x-y=8$ (2)

Eq. (1)+Eq. (2) $\Rightarrow 3x=21 \Rightarrow x=7$, $y=x-8=-1$ from Eq. (2)

  Answer $x=7, y=-1$ (2 marks)

4 Show, using algebra, that the sum of any 4 consecutive integers is always even.

a is the first integer.

The sum of the 4 consecutive integers are:

$a+(a+1)+(a+2)+(a+3) = 4a+6 = 2(2a+3)$

$2(2a+3)$ is always even for any integer a.

∴ The sum of any 4 consecutive integers is always even.

                 (2 marks)

5(a) $x^2 - 4x - 12 \leq 0$

Work out the range of values of x

$x^2 - 4x - 12 \leq 0 \Rightarrow (x+2)(x-6) \leq 0 \Rightarrow -2 \leq x \leq 6$

  Answer $-2 \leq x \leq 6$ (2 marks)

10

5(b) Solve $x^4 = 4x^2$

$x^4 = 4x^2 \Rightarrow x^2(x^2-4) \Rightarrow x^2(x-2)(x+2) = 0 \Rightarrow x = 0, 2$ or -2

Answer $-2, 0, 2$ (3 marks)

6   A bag contains blue, green and white balls. The ratio of blue balls to green balls is 2:3. The ratio of green balls to white balls is 2:5.

Work out the smallest possible number of balls in the bag.

Blue:Green=2:3=4:6

Green:White=2:5=6:15

Blue:Green:White=4:6:15

∴ The smallest possible number of balls in the bag is

$4+6+15 = 25$

Answer   25   (3 marks)

7   Sarah flew on a plane from Beijing to London.

The plane flew a distance of 8400 km.

The flight time was 10 hours and 15 minutes.

Work out the average speed of the plane in kilometres per hour.

Give your answer to 1 decimal place.

The average speed is $\dfrac{8400}{10+\dfrac{15}{60}} = 819.5$

Answer   819.5 km/h   (2 marks)

8   An antiques dealer buys a vase for £400. He sells the vase for 50% more than the price he paid for it.

8(a) For how much does the dealer sell the vase?

$400 \times (1+50\%) = 600$

Answer   £600   (2 marks)

8(b) It costs the dealer £60 to restore the vase before he sell it. Calculate the amount of profit the deal made.

$600 - 400 - 60 = 140$

Answer   £140   (3 marks)

13

8(c) Calculate this profit as a percentage of the price the dealer paid for the vase.

$$\frac{140}{400} = 0.35 = 35\%$$

Answer   35%   (2 marks)

9   P is directly proportional to Q^2 where $Q > 0$. $P = 900$ when $Q = 15$.

9(a) Find a formula for P in terms of Q.

$P = kQ^2$ where k is a constant.

$$k = \frac{P}{Q^2} = \frac{900}{15^2} = 4$$

$\therefore P = 4Q^2$

Answer $P = 4Q^2$ (2 marks)

9(b) Find the value of Q when $P = 25$.

$$P = 4Q^2 \Rightarrow Q = \pm\sqrt{\frac{P}{4}}$$

$\because Q > 0$, clearly the negative answer is not suitable here.

$$Q = \sqrt{\frac{P}{4}} = \sqrt{\frac{25}{4}} = 2.5$$

Answer   2.5   (2 marks)

10   Rearrange $y = \sqrt[3]{\frac{2(w-x)}{x}}$ to make x the subject.

$$y = \sqrt[3]{\frac{2(w-x)}{x}} \Rightarrow y^3 x = 2w - 2x \Rightarrow x = \frac{2w}{y^3 + 2}$$

Answer $x = \dfrac{2w}{y^3 + 2}$ (3 marks)

11 Solid **A** and Solid **B** are mathematically similar.

Solid **A** has a volume of 728 cm³

Solid **B** has a volume of 5824 cm³

Solid **A** has surface area 384 cm²

Calculate the surface area of solid **B**.

The surface area of solid **B** can be calculated as follows:

$$\sqrt[3]{\frac{\text{Volume B}}{\text{Volume A}}} = \sqrt{\frac{\text{Area B}}{\text{Area A}}} \Rightarrow \text{Area B} = \left(\sqrt[3]{\frac{\text{Volume B}}{\text{Volume A}}}\right)^2 \times \text{Area A}$$

$$\left(\sqrt[3]{\frac{5824}{728}}\right)^2 \times 384 = 1536$$

Answer   1536 cm²   (3 marks)

12    $f(x) = \dfrac{1}{\sqrt{x+3}}$

12(a) State the range of values of x which must be excluded from the domain of $f(x)$

$x + 3 \leq 0 \Rightarrow x \leq -3$

Answer $x \leq -3$ (3 marks)

12(b) $g(x) = 3x$

Calculate $fg(2)$

$fg(2) = f(3 \times 2) = f(6) = \dfrac{1}{\sqrt{6+3}} = \dfrac{1}{3}$

Answer $\dfrac{1}{3}$ (3 marks)

13(a) A cuboid has the following dimensions:

Length 250 mm, measured to the nearest 10 mm

Breadth 150 mm, measured to the nearest 10 mm

Height 60 mm, measured to the nearest 10 mm.

Calculate the greatest possible volume of the cuboid.

The greatest possible volume of the cuboid is:

$(250+5) \times (150+5) \times (60+5) = 2569125$

Answer   2569125 mm^3 (3 marks)

13(b) Another cuboid has a volume of 20000 mm^3, measured to the nearest 100 mm^3. The area of its base (length $\times$ breadth) is 120 mm^2, measured to the nearest 10 mm^2.

Calculate the smallest possible height of this cuboid.

Give your answer to 3 significant figures.

The smallest possible height of this cuboid is:

$\dfrac{20000-50}{120+5} = 160$

Answer   160 mm   (3 marks)

14   *ABCD* is a kite.

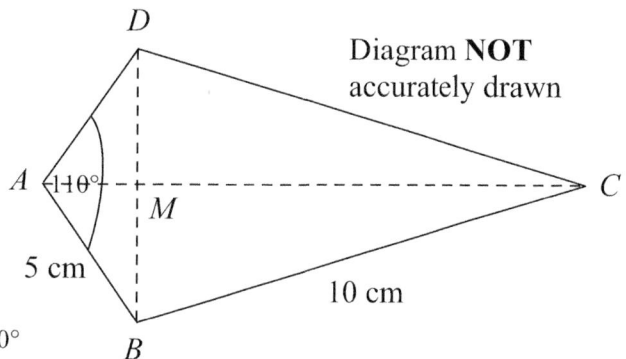

Diagram **NOT** accurately drawn

AB = 5 cm, *BC* = 10 cm, ∠*BAD* = 110°

Calculate the area of kite *ABCD*.

Give your answer to 3 significant figures.

Draw the lines *AC* and *BD*. They intersects at *M*. *AC* is perpendicular to *BD*.

In the right-angled triangle *AMB*, $AM = AB \times \cos \angle MAB = 5 \times \cos \dfrac{110°}{2} = 2.868$,

$BM = AB \times \sin \angle MAB = 5 \times \sin \dfrac{110°}{2} = 4.096$

In the right-angled triangle *BMC*, $MC = \sqrt{BC^2 - BM^2} = \sqrt{10^2 - 4.096^2} = 9.123$

The area of kite *ABCD* is

$\dfrac{BD \times AC}{2} = \dfrac{2BM \times (AM + MC)}{2} = BM \times (AM + MC) = 4.096 \times (2.868 + 9.123) = 49.1$

Answer   49.1 cm²   (3 marks)

15 The tent shown in the diagram has a base that is 2.5 m wide and 4.0 m long. The height of the tent is 1.5 m. The ends are isosceles triangles $AE = ED$, $BF = FC$, and perpendicular to the base.

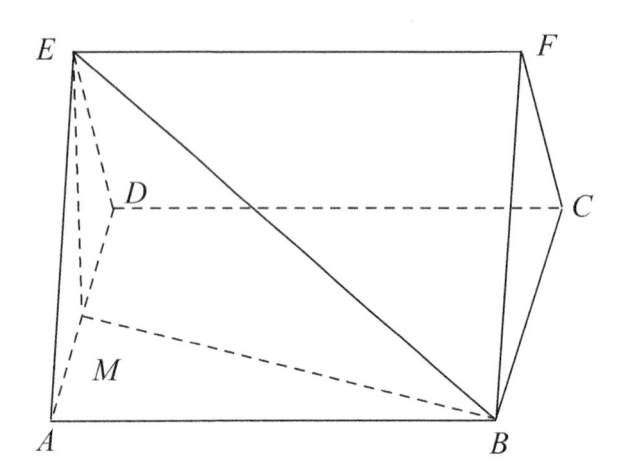

15(a) Work out the length of *BE*.

Give your answer to 3 significant figures.

M is midpoint of *AD*, *EM* is perpendicular to *MB*.

In the right-angled triangles *EAB* and *AME*,

$$BE = \sqrt{AE^2 + AB^2} = \sqrt{EM^2 + AM^2 + AB^2} = \sqrt{1.5^2 + (\frac{2.5}{2})^2 + 4^2} = 4.45$$

Answer   4.45 m   (3 marks)

15(b) Work out the angle between *BE* and *ABCD*.

Give your answer to 1 decimal place.

The angle between *BE* and *ABCD* is equal to ∠*EBM*

In the right-angled triangle *BME*,

$$\angle EAM = \sin^{-1}\frac{EM}{BE} = \sin^{-1}\frac{1.5}{4.45} = 19.7°$$

Answer   19.7°   (3 marks)

16   The diagram shows a regular pentagon *ABCDE*. The perimeter of the pentagon is 50 cm.

Calculate the area of the pentagon.

Give your answer to 2 decimal places.

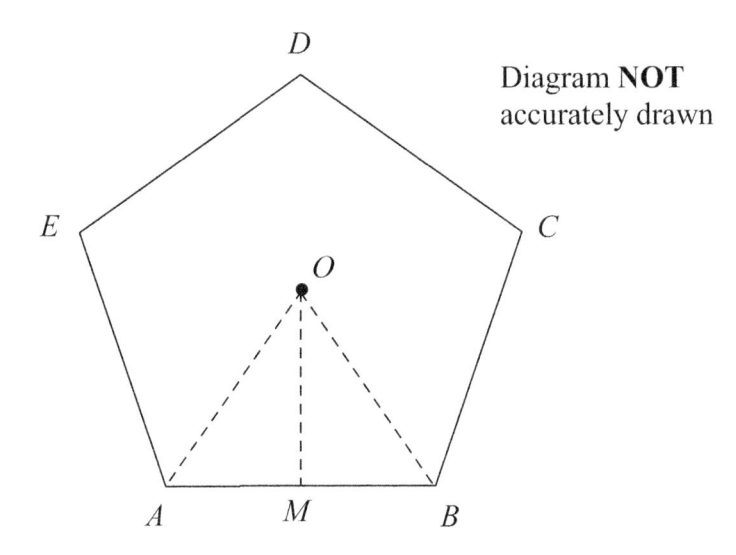

Diagram **NOT** accurately drawn

O is the centre of the pentagon. *M* is the midpoint of *AB*. ∴ *OM* is perpendicular to *AB*.

$$\angle EAB = \frac{(5-2)}{5} \times 180° = 108°, \quad \angle OAM = \frac{\angle EAB}{2} = 54°$$

$$AB = \frac{50}{5} = 10, \quad OM = AM \times \tan \angle OAM = \frac{AB}{2} \times \tan 54° = 5 \times \tan 54°$$

The area of the pentagon is

$$5 \times \frac{AB \times OM}{2} = 5 \times \frac{10 \times 5 \times \tan 54°}{2} = 172.05$$

Answer   172.05 cm² (3 marks)

17   *ABCD* is a cyclic quadrilateral. ∠*DAB* = 2×∠*CDT* , *DT* is a tangent to the circle.

Prove that triangle *BCD* is isosceles.

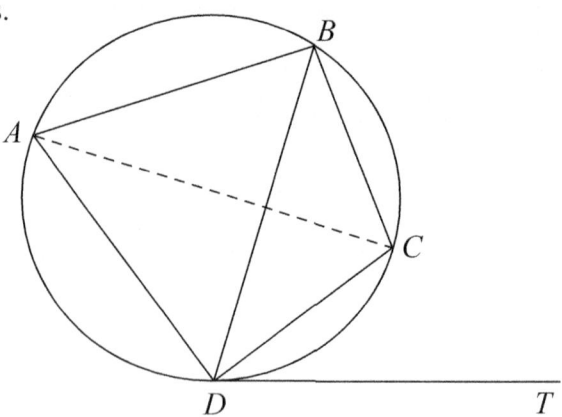

Draw line *AC* on the graph.

DT is a tangent to the circle , ∠*CDT* = ∠*CBD* = ∠*DAC*   (1)

∠*DAB* = 2×∠*CDT* ⇒ ∠*DAC* + ∠*CAB* = 2×∠*CDT*   (2)

From Eqs. (1) and (2), ∠*CAB* = ∠*CDT* = ∠*CBD*   (3)

∠*CDB* = ∠*CAB* , as they have the same chord.   (4)

From Eqs. (3) and (4), ∠*CDB* = ∠*CBD*

∴ *BC* = *CD* , triangle *BCD* is isosceles   (3 marks)

18 The histogram shows information about the marks, in percentage, that some students took maths challenge.

20 students have the marks of less than 20%.

Work out the total number of students.

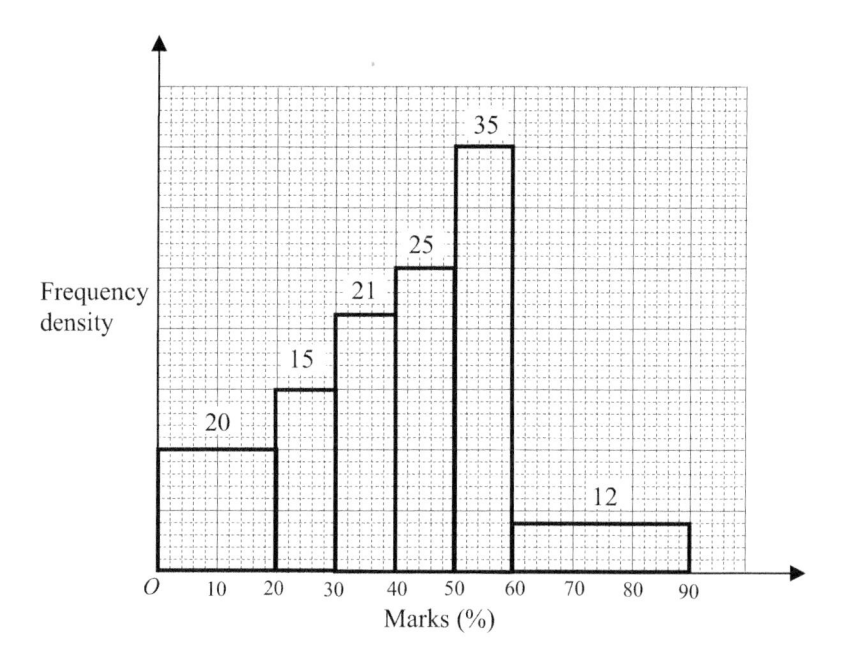

As 20 students have the marks of less than 20%, the number of students can be calculated from the histogram, and labelled on the graph above for the different range of marks.

The total number of students $= 20 + 15 + 21 + 25 + 35 + 12 = 128$

Answer   128   (5 marks)

19 Jack has 5 black pens, 2 blue pens and 3 red pens in his school bag. He takes two pens from his bag at random.

19(a) What is the probability that both pens are red?

The fully probability tree diagram is labelled below.

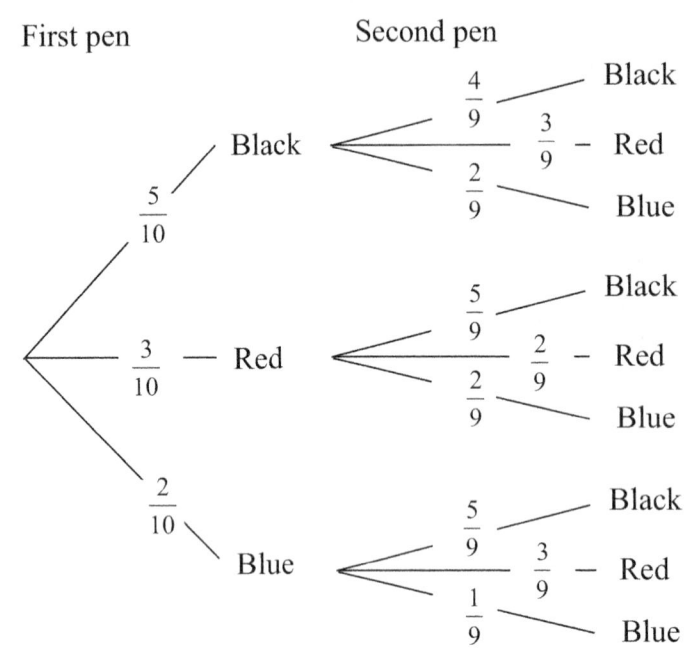

First pen   Second pen

$\frac{5}{10}$ — Black
- $\frac{4}{9}$ — Black
- $\frac{3}{9}$ — Red
- $\frac{2}{9}$ — Blue

$\frac{3}{10}$ — Red
- $\frac{5}{9}$ — Black
- $\frac{2}{9}$ — Red
- $\frac{2}{9}$ — Blue

$\frac{2}{10}$ — Blue
- $\frac{5}{9}$ — Black
- $\frac{3}{9}$ — Red
- $\frac{1}{9}$ — Blue

The probability, that both pens are red, is:

$$\frac{3}{10} \times \frac{2}{9} = \frac{1}{15}$$

Answer $\frac{1}{15}$ (3 marks)

19(b) What is the probability that just one pen is red?

From the fully probability tree diagram above, the probability, that just one pen is red, is:

$$\frac{5}{10} \times \frac{3}{9} + \frac{3}{10} \times \frac{5}{9} + \frac{3}{10} \times \frac{2}{9} + \frac{2}{10} \times \frac{3}{9} = \frac{7}{15}$$

Answer $\frac{7}{15}$ (3 marks)

20   There are 100 students in Year 10.

All students study at least one of art, drama and music.

8 of the students study art and drama and music.

24 of the students study art and drama.

36 of the students study art and music.

13 of the students study drama and music.

68 of the students study art.

55 of the students study music.

20(a)   Draw a Venn diagram to show this information.

Firstly fill the number of elements in the following order:

n(Music ∩ Art ∩ Drama) =8, "8" is in the region which sets Music, Art and Drama share.

n(Art ∩ Drama) = 24=8+16, "16" is in the region which only sets Art and Drama share.

n(Art ∩ Music) = 36=8+28, "28" is in the region which only sets Art and Music share.

n(Drama ∩ Music) = 13=8+5, "5" is in the region which only sets Drama and Music share.

Secondly fill the remaining number of elements of sets *A*, *B* and *C*, on the diagram.

n(Art)=68=16+8+28+16, the second "16" is in Art region which does not share with sets Drama and Music.

n(Music) = 55=5+8+28+14, "14" is in Music region which does not share with sets Art and Drama.

n(Drama)=100- n((Drama)')=100-16-28-14=42,

n(Drama)=42=8+5+16+13, "13" is in Drama region which does not share with sets Art and Music.

(3 marks)

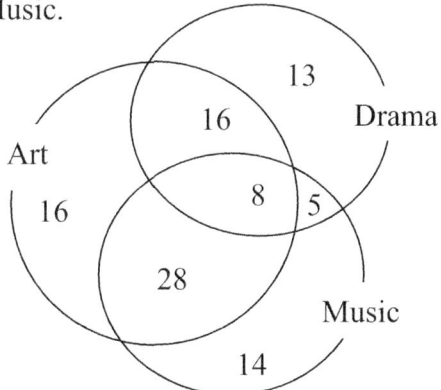

20(b) One of the 100 students is selected at random. Find the probability that this student studies drama but not art.

$$\frac{13+5}{100} = \frac{9}{50}$$

Answer $\frac{9}{50}$ (3 marks)

21 OABC is a parallelogram. BCD is a straight line. BD=3BC. M is the midpoint of OC.

$\vec{OA} = \mathbf{x}$, $\vec{AB} = \mathbf{y}$.

Show by a vector method that AM is parallel to OD.

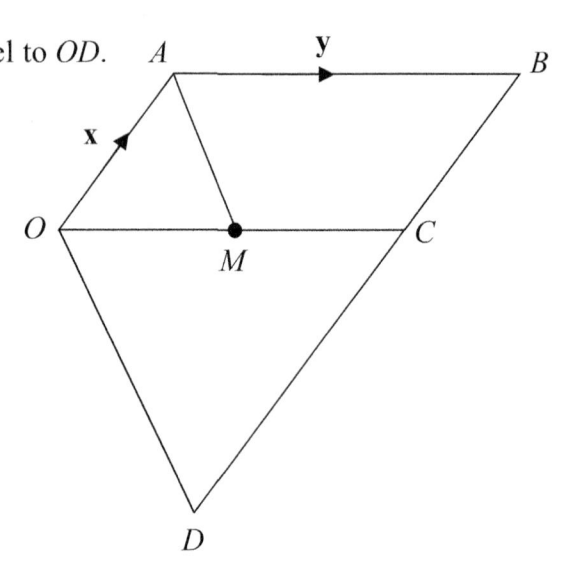

OABC is a parallelogram. BCD is a straight line $\Rightarrow$ CB=OA

BD=3BC $\Rightarrow$ $\vec{DB} = 3\mathbf{x}$

M is the midpoint of OC $\Rightarrow$ $\vec{OM} = \frac{\vec{AB}}{2} = \frac{\mathbf{y}}{2}$

$\vec{OD} = \vec{OA} + \vec{AB} - \vec{DB} = \mathbf{x} + \mathbf{y} - 3\mathbf{x} = \mathbf{y} - 2\mathbf{x}$

$\vec{AM} = \vec{OM} - \vec{OA} = \frac{\mathbf{y}}{2} - \mathbf{x} = \frac{\vec{OD}}{2}$

∴ AM is parallel to OD (3 marks)

22 Line L has gradient 2 and passes through (2,1).

Work out the equation of the line.

Give your answer in the form $y = mx + c$.

$y - 1 = 2(x - 2) \Rightarrow y = 2x - 3$

Answer $y = 2x - 3$ (2 marks)

23 The curve with equation $y = 4x^2 + \dfrac{1}{x}$ has one stationary point.

Find the coordinates of this stationary point.

Show your working clearly.

$\dfrac{dy}{dx} = 8x - x^{-2}$, $8x - x^{-2} = 0 \Rightarrow x = \dfrac{1}{2} \Rightarrow y = 4x^2 + \dfrac{1}{x} = 3$

∴ The coordinates of this stationary point are $(\dfrac{1}{2}, 3)$

Answer $(\dfrac{1}{2}, 3)$ (2 marks)

24 Here is the graph of $y = 2(x-2)^2 - 1$ for values of x from 0 to 4.

24(a) Use the Use the graph to find estimates for the solutions of $2(x-2)^2 - 1 = 0$.

Give your answers to 1 decimal place.

The graph intersects the x-axis about $x = 1.3$ and $x = 2.7$

Answer   1.3 , 2.7   (2 marks)

24(b) Use the graph to find estimates for the solutions of the simultaneous equations

(i) $y = 2(x-2)^2 - 1$.

(ii) $y = 2x - 2$

Draw the line $y = 2x - 2$ on the graph $\Rightarrow x = 1.2$, $y = 0.4$ or $x = 3.8$, $y = 5.6$

Answer $x = 1.2, y = 0.4$; $x = 3.8, y = 5.6$

(2 marks)

24(c) By drawing a suitable linear graph on the grid, work out approximate solutions of

$2x^2 - 9x + 8 = 0$.

Give your answers to 1 decimal place.

$y = 2(x-2)^2 - 1$ (1)

$2x^2 - 9x + 8 = 0$ (2)

Eq. (1) + Eq. (2) $\Rightarrow y = x - 1$

Draw the line $y = x - 1$ on the graph $\Rightarrow x = 1.2$ or $x = 3.3$

Answer   1.2 , 3.3   (4 marks)

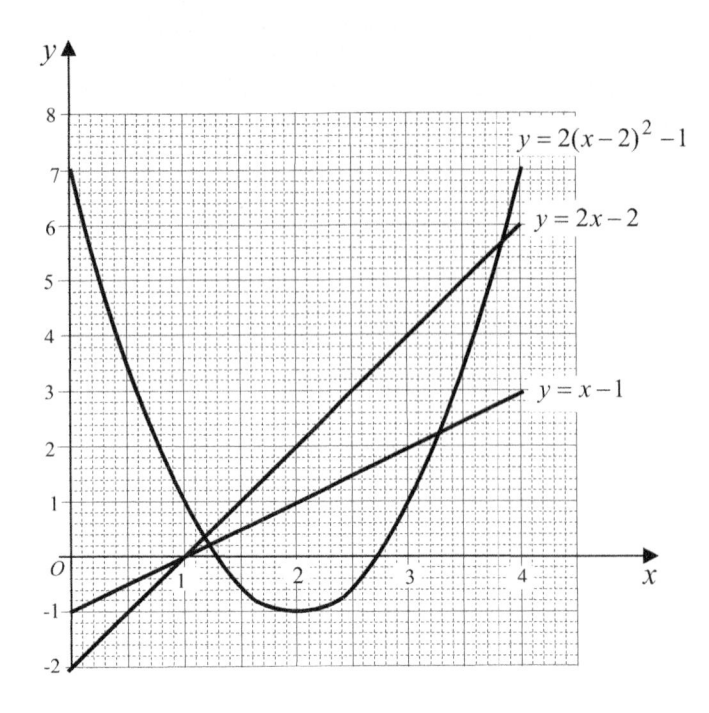

25 The diagram shows the graph of $y = \sin x$ for $0° \leq x \leq 360°$

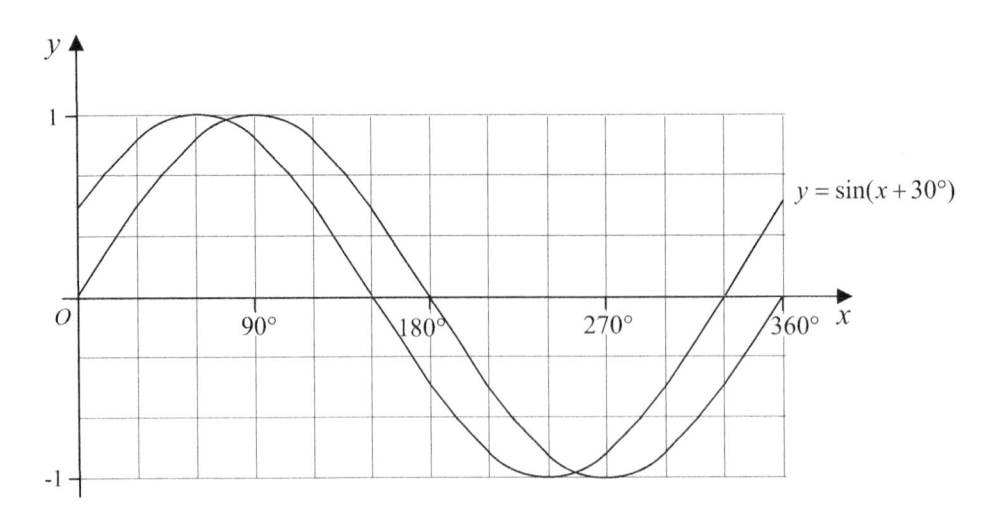

25(a) On the grid above, sketch the graph of $y = \sin(x + 30°)$ for $0° \leq x \leq 360°$

As shown on the graph. (3 marks)

25(b) The graph of $y = \sin(x + 30°) + 2$ has a minimum at point A for $0° \leq x \leq 360°$. Write down the coordinates of A.

$y = \sin(x + 30°)$ has a minimum at $(240°, -1)$, for $0° \leq x \leq 360°$

$\therefore y = \sin(x + 30°) + 2$ has a minimum at $(240°, 1)$

The coordinates of A are $(240°, 1)$

Answer $(240°, 1)$ (3 marks)

Paper 3 solutions

1 Simplify $p^3 \times p^6$

$p^3 \times p^6 = p^{3+6} = p^9$

Answer $\quad p^9 \quad$ (3 marks)

2 Simplify fully $\dfrac{9x}{(x+2)(x-4)} - \dfrac{3}{x+2}$

$\dfrac{9x}{(x+2)(x-4)} - \dfrac{3}{x+2} = \dfrac{9x}{(x+2)(x-4)} - \dfrac{3(x-4)}{(x+2)(x-4)} = \dfrac{6(x+2)}{(x+2)(x-4)} = \dfrac{6}{x-4}$

Answer $\quad \dfrac{6}{x-4} \quad$ (3 marks)

3 Write down the value of m^0, where $m \neq 0$

Answer $\quad 1 \quad$ (3 marks)

4 Write as a single power of x

$\left(\dfrac{x^{\frac{4}{3}} \times x^{\frac{5}{3}}}{x}\right)^3$

$\left(\dfrac{x^{\frac{4}{3}} \times x^{\frac{5}{3}}}{x}\right)^3 = \left(x^{\frac{4}{3}-1+\frac{5}{3}}\right)^3 = (x^2)^3 = x^{2\times 3} = x^6$

Answer $\quad x^6 \quad$ (3 marks)

5 Factorise fully $(x^2 - 16) - (x+4)^2 + (x+4)(x+1)$

$(x^2 - 16) - (x+4)^2 + (x+4)(x+1)$
$= (x+4)(x-4) - (x+4)^2 + (x+4)(x+1)$
$= (x+4)(x-4-x-4+x+1)$
$= (x+4)(x-7)$

Answer $\quad (x+4)(x-7) \quad$ (3 marks)

15

6   Solve $(1-\sqrt{x})^{\frac{1}{3}} = -2$

$(1-\sqrt{x})^{\frac{1}{3}} = -2 \Rightarrow 1-\sqrt{x} = -8 \Rightarrow \sqrt{x} = 9 \Rightarrow x = 81$

Answer   81   (3 marks)

7   $x^2 + 4x - 5 \equiv (x+a)^2 + b$

Work out the values of a and b.

$x^2 + 4x - 5 = (x+2)^2 - 4 - 5 = (x+2)^2 - 9$

$\therefore a = 2, \ b = -9$

Answer $a = 2, \ b = -9$ (3 marks)

8   $x:y = 3:2$ and $a:b = 5x:3y$

Work out $a:b$

Give your answer in its simplest form.

$\dfrac{a}{b} = \dfrac{5x}{3y} = \dfrac{5}{3} \times \dfrac{x}{y} = \dfrac{5}{3} \times \dfrac{3}{2} = \dfrac{5}{2}$

Answer $5:2$ (3 marks)

9   Rearrange $p = \dfrac{y}{y-2}$ to make y the subject.

$p = \dfrac{y}{y-2} \Rightarrow p(y-2) = y \Rightarrow y(p-1) = 2p \Rightarrow y = \dfrac{2p}{p-1}$

Answer $y = \dfrac{2p}{p-1}$ (3 marks)

10   a is a positive integer, show that $\sqrt{2a}(\sqrt{8a} + a\sqrt{2a})$ is always a multiple of 2.

$\sqrt{2a}(\sqrt{8a} + a\sqrt{2a}) = \sqrt{2a}(2\sqrt{2a} + a\sqrt{2a}) = 4a + 2a^2 = 2(2a + a^2)$

$\therefore \sqrt{2a}(\sqrt{8a} + a\sqrt{2a})$ is always a multiple of 2

(2 marks)

11   The function $f(x)$ is defined as $f(x) = \sqrt{x^2 - 36}$.

State the range of values of x which must be excluded from the domain of $f(x)$

$x^2 - 36 < 0 \Rightarrow (x-6)(x+6) < 0 \Rightarrow -6 < x < 6$

Answer $-6 < x < 6$ (3 marks)

12   Solve $3x^2 + 2x - 6 = 0$

Give your solutions to 3 significant figures.

$x = \dfrac{-2 \pm \sqrt{2^2 - 4 \times 3 \times (-6)}}{2 \times 3} = \dfrac{-1 \pm \sqrt{19}}{3} \Rightarrow x = 1.12 \text{ or } x = -1.79$.

Answer   1.12, -1.79   (3 marks)

13   A clothes shop has a sale.

In the sale, normal prices are reduced by 15%.

13(a)   The normal price of a tie is £12.

Work out the sale price of the tie.

$12 \times (1 - 15\%) = 10.20$

Answer   £10.20   (3 marks)

13(b)   The price of a jumper is reduced by £6.00 in the sale.

Work out the normal price of the jumper.

$x \times 15\% = 6 \Rightarrow x = 40$

Answer   £40.00   (2 marks)

14    $y = x^3 - 3x^2 - 9x + 5$

14(a) Find $\dfrac{dy}{dx}$

$\dfrac{dy}{dx} = 3x^2 - 6x - 9$

   Answer $3x^2 - 6x - 9$ (2 marks)

14(b) The curve with equation $y = x^3 - 3x^2 - 9x + 5$ has two turning points.

Work out the coordinates of these two turning points.

Show your working clearly.

$\dfrac{dy}{dx} = 0 \Rightarrow 3x^2 - 6x - 9 = 0 \Rightarrow 3(x-3)(x+1) = 0 \Rightarrow x = -1, \ x = 3$

when $x = -1$, $y = (-1)^3 - 3\times(-1)^2 - 9\times(-1) + 5 = 10$

when $x = 3$, $y = (3)^3 - 3\times 3^2 - 9\times 3 + 5 = -22$

The coordinates of these two turning points are (-1,10) and (3,-22).

   Answer   (-1,10) and (3,-22)   (4 marks)

15   ξ is a universal set.

$\xi = \{1,2,3,4,5,6,7,8,9,10,11,12,13,14,15\}$

$A = \{3,4,5,8,13,15\}$, $B = \{4,6,8,9,11,12\}$, $C = \{2,3,4,7,9,11,13\}$

15(a) Complete the Venn diagram.

Firstly fill the members of these sets in the following order: $A \cap B \cap C = \{4\}$,

$A \cap B = \{4,8\}$, $A \cap C = \{3,4,13\}$, $B \cap C = \{4,9,11\}$, on the diagram.

Secondly fill the remaining members of sets *A*, *B* and *C*, on the diagram.

Thirdly fill the remaining members of set ξ, on the diagram.

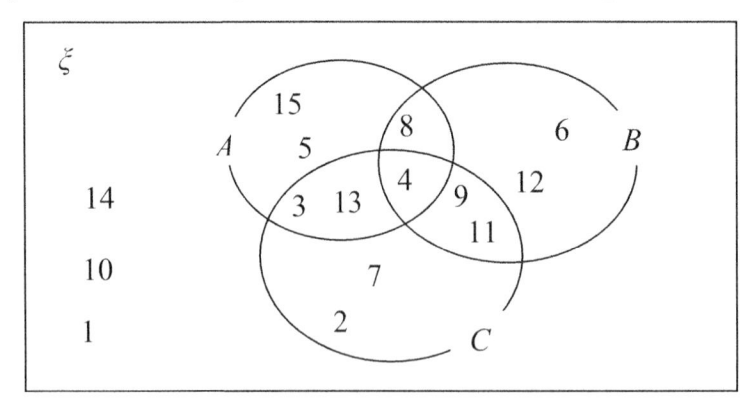

(4 marks)

15 (b) List the members of the set $(A \cup B)' \cap C$

$(A \cup B)' \cap C = \{2,7\}$

Answer   2,7   (2 marks)

16   A sphere and a cone have the same volume. The base of the cone and the sphere have the same radius r cm.

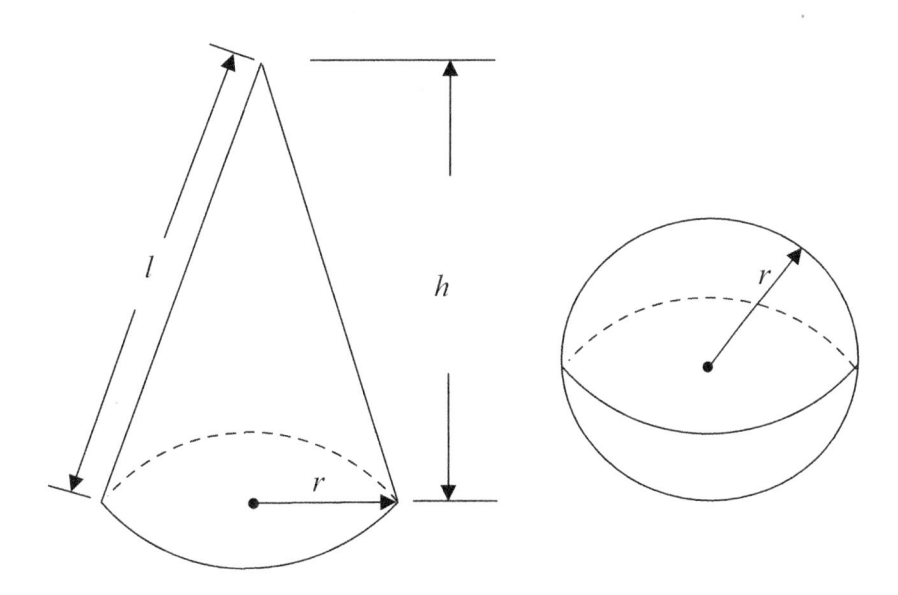

Work out the curved surface area of cone in terms of r.

The sphere and the cone have the same volume,

$\therefore \dfrac{1}{3}\pi r^2 h = \dfrac{4}{3}\pi r^3 \Rightarrow h = 4r$ where h is the height of the cone.

l is the slant height,

$l = \sqrt{h^2 + r^2} = \sqrt{(4r)^2 + r^2} = \sqrt{17}\, r$

$\therefore$ The curved surface area of cone is:

$\pi r l = \pi r \times \sqrt{17}\, r = \sqrt{17}\, \pi r^2$

Answer $\sqrt{17}\, \pi r^2$ cm^2 (4 marks)

17 QPRS is a cyclic quadrilateral. C is the centre of the circle. ∠QCM = ∠SMR = 80°.

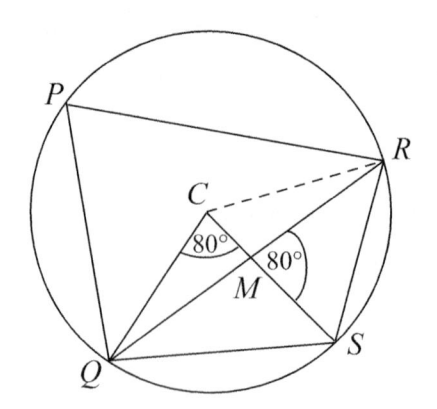

Work out the value of ∠QPR

∠CMQ = ∠SMR = 80°, ∠CQM = 180° − ∠CMQ − ∠QCM = 180° − 80° − 80° = 20°

Draw line CR

C is the centre of the circle ⇒ CQR is an isosceles triangles.

∠CQM = ∠CRM = 20°,

∠RCQ = 180° − ∠CQM − ∠CRM = 180° − 20° − 20° = 140°

∠RCQ = 2∠QPR (Angle at the centre is double the angle at the circumference.)

∴ ∠QPR = $\frac{1}{2}$∠RCQ = $\frac{1}{2}$ × 140° = 70°

Answer   70°   (4 marks)

18 Here are a trapezium and a right-angled triangle.

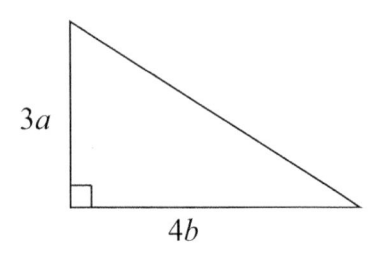

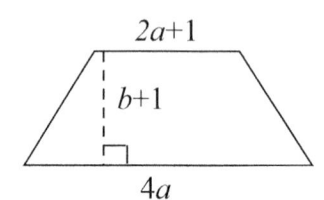

Diagram **NOT** accurately drawn

The area of the triangle is equal to the area of trapezium.

Find an expression for a in terms of b, where $b>1$

$\frac{3a \times 4b}{2} = \frac{2a+1+4a}{2}(b+1) \Rightarrow a = \frac{b+1}{6b-6}$

Answer $a = \frac{b+1}{6b-6}$ (4 marks)

8

19   Here is a list of members written in order of size.

   3   6   x   12   y   16

   The numbers have a median of 11 and have a mean of 10.

   Find the values of x and y.

   The numbers have a median of 11 and have a mean of 10.

   ∴ $\frac{x+12}{2} = 11 \Rightarrow x = 10$

   $\frac{3+6+x+y+12+16}{6} = 10 \Rightarrow y = 13$

   Answer $x = 10$, $y = 13$ (2 marks)

20   A box contains toy cars. Each car is red or black or blue or silver.

   Jack takes a car at random from the box.

   The table shows the probabilities that Jack takes a red car or a blue car or a black car or silver.

20(a)   Work out the probability that Jack takes a silver car.

   The probability that Jack takes a silver car is:

   $1 - 0.50 - 0.30 - 0.075 = 0.125$

   Answer   0.125   (2 marks)

20(b)   Jack adds 50 black cars into the box. The following table shows the probabilities that Jack takes a red car or a blue car or a black car or silver after he adds 50 black cars into the box.

Colour of car	Probability
red	0.40
blue	0.24
black	0.26
silver	0.10

   Work out the total number of cars in the box originally.

   The total number of cars in the box originally is x

   $0.26(x+50) - 0.075x = 50 \Rightarrow x = 200$

   Answer   200   (4 marks)

21 Line *L* passes through (6,1) and (3,3).

Work out the equation of the line.

Give your answer in the form $ax+by=c$, where *a, b* and *c* are integers.

$$y-3=\frac{3-1}{3-6}\times(x-3) \Rightarrow y-3=-\frac{2}{3}x+2 \Rightarrow 2x+3y=15$$

Answer $\quad 2x+3y=15 \quad$ (2 marks)

22 The graph shows two lines. *L2* is a reflection of *L1*: $y=2-2x$ through $x=1$.

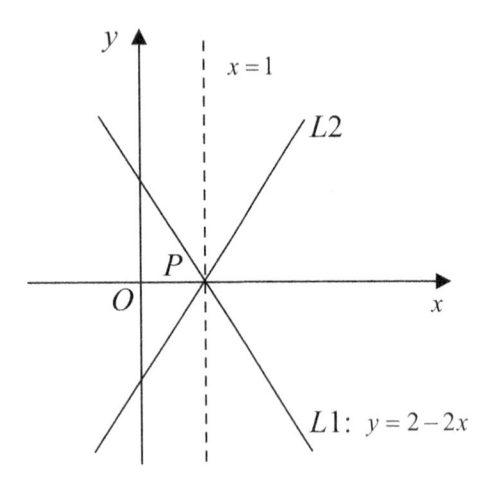

Work out the equation of *L2*.

Give your answer in the form $y=mx+c$.

L1: $y=2-2x \Rightarrow P(1,0)$.

L2 passes through points *P* with gradient 2.

The equation of *L2* is:

$y=2(x-1) \Rightarrow y=2x-2$

Answer $\quad y=2x-2 \quad$ (2 marks)

23   The diagram shows a circle, centre C. TP is a tangent to the circle and intersects the x-axis at T.

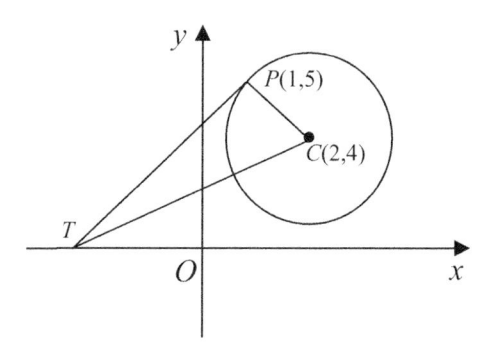

Work out the length of TP

TP is a tangent to the circle, ∴ TP is perpendicular to CP

The gradient of CP is $\frac{5-4}{1-2} = -1$, the gradient of TP is 1

The equation of TP is $y - 5 = x - 1 \Rightarrow y = x + 4$

When $y = 0$, $x = -4$ for line TP, $y = x + 4$.

∴ The coordinates of T are (-4,0).

The length of TP is:

$$\sqrt{(T_x - P_x)^2 + (T_y - P_y)^2} = \sqrt{(-4-1)^2 + (0-5)^2} = 5\sqrt{2}$$

Answer $5\sqrt{2}$ units   (3 marks)

24(a) Describe fully the single transformation that maps shape **P** onto shape **Q**.

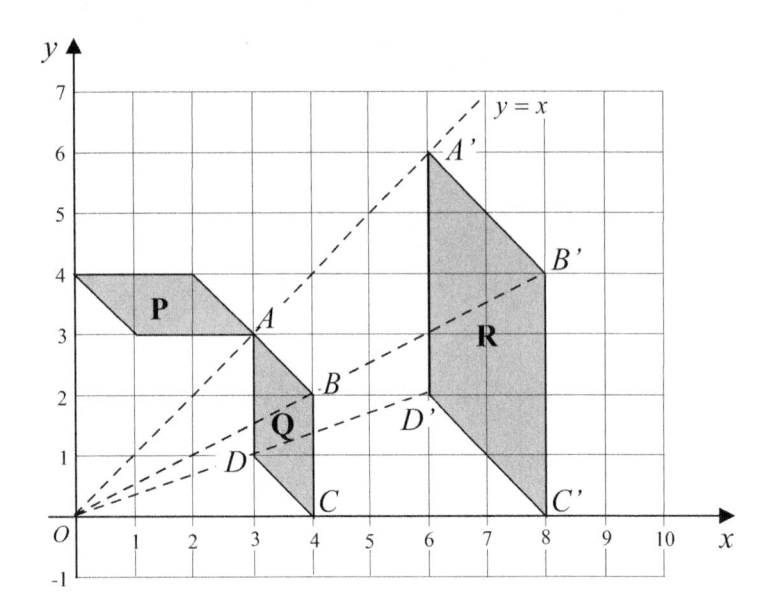

Answer   Reflection in the line $y = x$.   (2 marks)

24(b) On the grid, enlarge shape **Q** with scale factor 2 and centre O.

To enlarge shape **Q** with scale factor 2 and centre O to get shape **R**, extend OA to A' so that OA' is twice OA to get the vertex A' of shape **R**. In the same way, get the other vertexes, B', C' and D' of shape **R**.

(5 marks)

25 Point *P* and vectors **a** and **b** are shown on the grid.

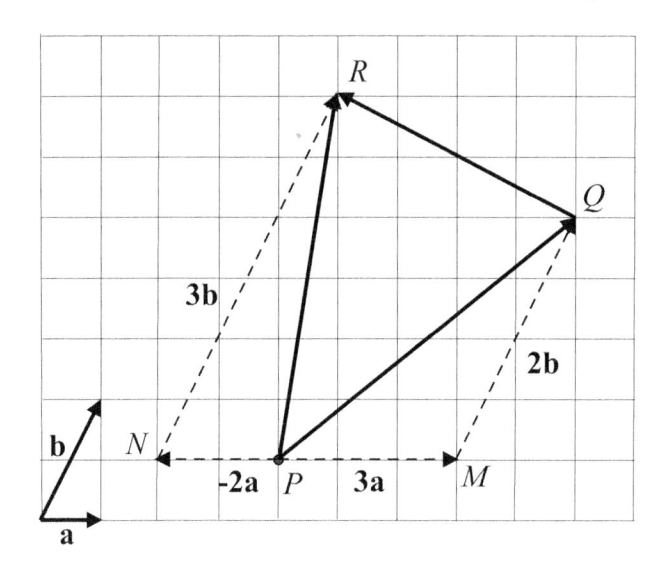

25(a) $\vec{PQ} = 3\mathbf{a} + 2\mathbf{b}$

On the grid, mark vector $\vec{PQ}$

Firstly from *P*, draw 3**a**, $\vec{PM} = 3\mathbf{a}$,

Secondly from *M*, draw 2**b**, $\vec{MQ} = 2\mathbf{b}$,

∴ $\vec{PQ} = \vec{PM} + \vec{MQ} = 3\mathbf{a} + 2\mathbf{b}$

$\vec{PQ}$ is as shown on the diagram. (5 marks)

25(b) $\vec{PR} = -2\mathbf{a} + 3\mathbf{b}$

On the grid, mark vector $\vec{PR}$

In the same method as part (a) above, draw $\vec{PN} = -2\mathbf{a}$, $\vec{NR} = 3\mathbf{b}$.

∴ $\vec{PR} = -2\mathbf{a} + 3\mathbf{b}$

$\vec{PR}$ is as shown on the diagram. (5 marks)

25(c) Find vector $\vec{QR}$, in terms of **a** and **b**.

$\vec{QR} = \vec{PR} - \vec{PQ} = -2\mathbf{a} + 3\mathbf{b} - (3\mathbf{a} + 2\mathbf{b}) = -5\mathbf{a} + \mathbf{b}$

Answer $-5\mathbf{a} + \mathbf{b}$ (4 marks)

14

Paper 4 solutions

1. Expand and Simplify $(x-2)(x-1)(x+1)$

    $(x-2)(x-1)(x+1) = (x-2)(x^2-1) = x^3-2x^2-x+2$

    Answer $\qquad x^3-2x^2-x+2 \qquad$ (2 marks)

2. Factorise fully $9x^4-36x^2$.

    $9x^4-36x^2 = 9x^2(x^2-4) = 9x^2(x-2)(x+2)$

    Answer $\qquad 9x^2(x-2)(x+2) \qquad$ (2 marks)

3. Simplify $\dfrac{x^2+4x+4}{x^2-2x-8}$

    $\dfrac{x^2+4x+4}{x^2-2x-8} = \dfrac{(x+2)^2}{(x+2)(x-4)} = \dfrac{x+2}{x-4}$

    Answer $\qquad \dfrac{x+2}{x-4} \qquad$ (3 marks)

4. 60% of p = 30% of q.

    Work out p as a percentage of q.

    $60\% p = 30\% q \Rightarrow p = \dfrac{1}{2}q \Rightarrow p = 50\% q$

    Answer $\qquad p = 50\% q \qquad$ (3 marks)

5. $x:y = 2:3$ and z is 30% of y.

    Work out $x:z$

    Give your answer in its simplest form.

    $\dfrac{x}{y} = \dfrac{2}{3}$ $\qquad$ (1)

    $z = 30\% y \Rightarrow \dfrac{y}{z} = \dfrac{100}{30} \Rightarrow \dfrac{y}{z} = \dfrac{10}{3}$ $\qquad$ (2)

    Eq. (1) × Eq. (2) $\Rightarrow \dfrac{x}{z} = \dfrac{20}{9}$

    Answer $\qquad 20:9 \qquad$ (3 marks)

13

6 The function $f(x)$ is defined as $f(x) = \dfrac{1}{x^2+8x+15}$.

State the values of x which must be excluded from the domain of $f(x)$

$x^2+8x+15 \neq 0 \Rightarrow (x+3)(x+5) \neq 0 \Rightarrow x \neq -3$ and $x \neq -5$

Answer   −5, −3   (2 marks)

7 $f(x) = 2\cos x - 2$ for $0° \leq x \leq 360°$

Work out the range of $f(x)$.

$-1 \leq \cos x \leq 1 \Rightarrow -2 \leq 2\cos x \leq 2 \Rightarrow -4 \leq 2\cos x - 2 \leq 0$

$\therefore -4 \leq f(x) \leq 0$

Answer $-4 \leq f(x) \leq 0$ (3 marks)

8 $g(x) = x^2 - 4$

The range of $g(x)$ is $g(x) \leq 5$

Work out the domain of $g(x)$.

$g(x) = x^2 - 4$, $g(x) \leq 5$

$\therefore x^2 - 4 \leq 5 \Rightarrow x^2 - 9 \leq 0 \Rightarrow (x-3)(x+3) \leq 0 \Rightarrow -3 \leq x \leq 3$

Answer $-3 \leq x \leq 3$ (3 marks)

9 $f(n) = n^2$ for all positive integer values of n.

Prove that $f(n+1) - f(n)$ is always odd.

$f(n+1) - f(n) = (n+1)^2 - n^2 = n^2 + 2n + 1 - n^2 = 2n + 1$

$2n$ is always even, $2n+1$ is always odd.

$\therefore f(n+1) - f(n)$ is always odd   (3 marks)

10 There are 20 boys and 10 girls in a class. They took maths challenge. The mean mark that the boys have is 65%, while the mean mark that the girls have is 62%. Work out the mean mark that the 30 children have.

$\dfrac{65\% \times 20 + 62\% \times 10}{30} = 64\%$

Answer   64%   (3 marks)

11 The 10th term of an arithmetic series, S, is 20. The sum of the first 10 terms of S is 290.

Find the 5th term of S.

Show your working clearly.

$a_n = a_1 + (n-1)d$

$\Rightarrow 20 = a_1 + 9d$ (1)

$S_n = \dfrac{n}{2}[2a_1 + (n-1)d] \Rightarrow 290 = \dfrac{10}{2}[2a_1 + 9d]$

$\Rightarrow 290 = 10a_1 + 45d$ (2)

$10 \times$ Eq. (1) - Eq. (2) $\Rightarrow -90 = 45d \Rightarrow d = -2$

From Eq. (1), $a_1 = 20 - 9d = 20 + 9 \times 2 = 38$

$a_5 = a_1 + 4d = 38 + 4 \times (-2) = 30$

Answer   30   (3 marks)

12 On 1 April 2018, the cost of 5 grams of gold was £200. The cost of gold increased by 2.5% from 1 April 2018 to 1 April 2019.

Work out the cost of 20 grams of gold on 1 April 2019.

The gold price on 1 April 2018: $\dfrac{£200}{5g} = £40/g$

The gold price on 1 April 2019: $£40/g(1+2.5\%) = £41/g$

The cost of 20 grams of gold on 1 April 2019: $£41/g \times 20g = £820$

(Alterative method: $200 \times (1+2.5\%) \times 4 = 820$)

Answer   £820   (3 marks)

13 Show that $3\dfrac{2}{5} \div 1\dfrac{9}{25} = 2\dfrac{1}{2}$

$3\dfrac{2}{5} \div 1\dfrac{9}{25} = \dfrac{\cancel{17}^{1}}{\cancel{5}_{1}} \times \dfrac{\cancel{25}^{5}}{\cancel{34}_{2}} = \dfrac{5}{2} = 2\dfrac{1}{2}$

$\therefore 3\dfrac{2}{5} \div 1\dfrac{9}{25} = 2\dfrac{1}{2}$

(3 marks)

14 Rationalise the denominator and simply fully $\dfrac{\sqrt{3}-1}{2-\sqrt{3}}$

$\dfrac{\sqrt{3}-1}{2-\sqrt{3}} = \dfrac{(\sqrt{3}-1)(2+\sqrt{3})}{(2-\sqrt{3})(2+\sqrt{3})} = 2\sqrt{3}+3-2-\sqrt{3} = \sqrt{3}+1$

Answer $\sqrt{3}+1$ (3 marks)

15 A car travels a distance of 62.5 km, correct to the nearest 0.5 km. The car takes 45.8 minutes correct to 1 decimal place.

Work out the lower bound for the average speed of the car.

Show your working clearly.

Give your answer in km/h correct to 1 decimal place.

62.25 km ≤ The distance that the car travelled < 62.75 km

45.75 min ≤ The time that the car took < 45.85 min.

∴ The lower bound for the average speed of the car is:

$\dfrac{62.25 \text{ km}}{45.85 \text{ min}} = 1.358 \text{ km/min} = 81.5 \text{ km/h}$

Answer 81.5 km/h (3 marks)

16 The diagram shows a trapezium

Work out the value of x

Give your answer to 1 decimal place.

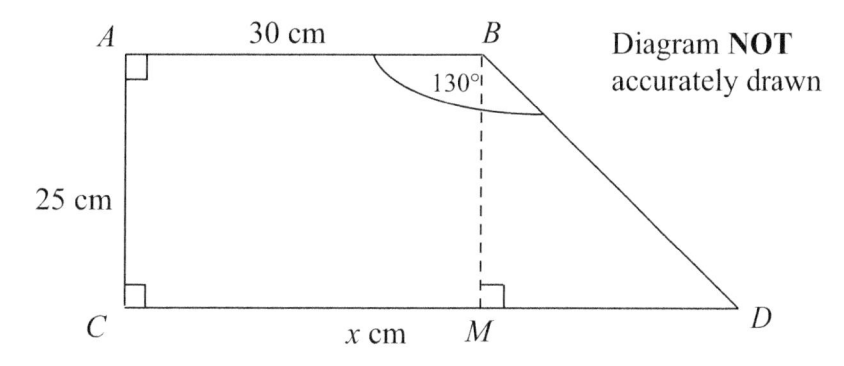

Diagram **NOT** accurately drawn

Draw line *BM*, which is perpendicular to *CD*.

$\angle DBM = 130° - 90° = 40°$

In the right-angled triangle *BMD*, $MD = BM \times \tan \angle DBM = 25 \times \tan 40°$

$x = CM + MD = 30 + 25 \times \tan 40° = 51.0$

Answer 51.0 (3 marks)

17   A circle touches all vertices of the square. The radius of the circle is 5 cm as shown.

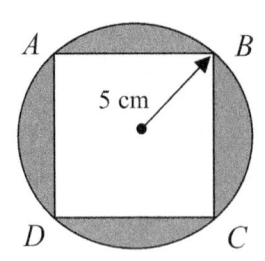

Work out the total shaded area.

Give your answer to 2 decimal places.

The total shaded area $= \pi r^2 - (\sqrt{2}r)^2 = \pi r^2 - 2r^2 = 25(\pi - 2) = 28.54$

Answer   28.54 cm²   (3 marks)

18   *ABCD* is a cyclic quadrilateral. *O* is the centre of the circle.

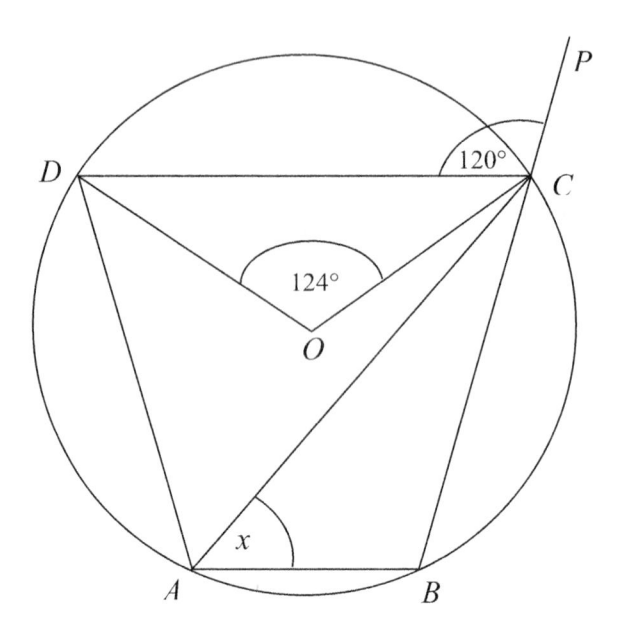

Work out the value of *x*.

ABCD is a cyclic quadrilateral, $\therefore \angle BAD + \angle BCD = 180°$

$\angle BCD + \angle PCD = 180°$, $\therefore \angle BAD = \angle PCD = 120°$

O is the centre of the circle, $\therefore \angle CAD = \dfrac{\angle COD}{2} = \dfrac{124°}{2} = 62°$

(The angle at the centre is twice the angle at the circumference.)

$x = \angle BAC = \angle BAD - \angle CAD = 120° - 62° = 58°$

Answer   58°   (4 marks)

19   The diagram shows a solid prism. The top *EFGH* is a rectangle of width 20 cm and length 30 cm, the base *ABCD* is rectangle of width 20 cm and length 50 cm. The line joining the centres of the top and the base is perpendicular to both and is 40 cm long. The prism is made from wood with density 0.0007 kg/cm³.

Work out the mass of the prism.

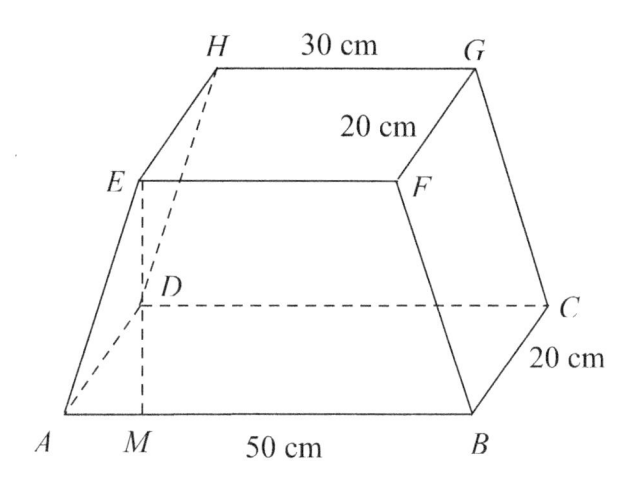

Draw a line *EM* which is perpendicular *AB*. *EM* = 40 cm.

The prism has a height of 20 cm and the cross section with a trapezium.

The volume of the prism is:

$\frac{EF + AB}{2} \times EM \times BC$

∴ The mass of the prism is

$\frac{EF + AB}{2} \times EM \times BC \times 0.0007 = \frac{30 + 50}{2} \times 40 \times 20 \times 0.0007 = 22.4$

Answer   22.4 kg   (4 marks)

20 The table shows information about the amount of money that 100 people spent in a shop.

Amount of money (£)	Frequency
$0 < m \leq 10$	6
$10 < m \leq 20$	15
$20 < m \leq 30$	22
$30 < m \leq 40$	35
$40 < m \leq 50$	16
$50 < m \leq 60$	6

20(a) Complete the cumulative frequency table

Amount of money (£)	Cumulative Frequency
$0 < m \leq 10$	6
$0 < m \leq 20$	21
$0 < m \leq 30$	43
$0 < m \leq 40$	78
$0 < m \leq 50$	94
$0 < m \leq 60$	100

(6 marks)

20(b) On the grid, draw a cumulative frequency graph for your table.

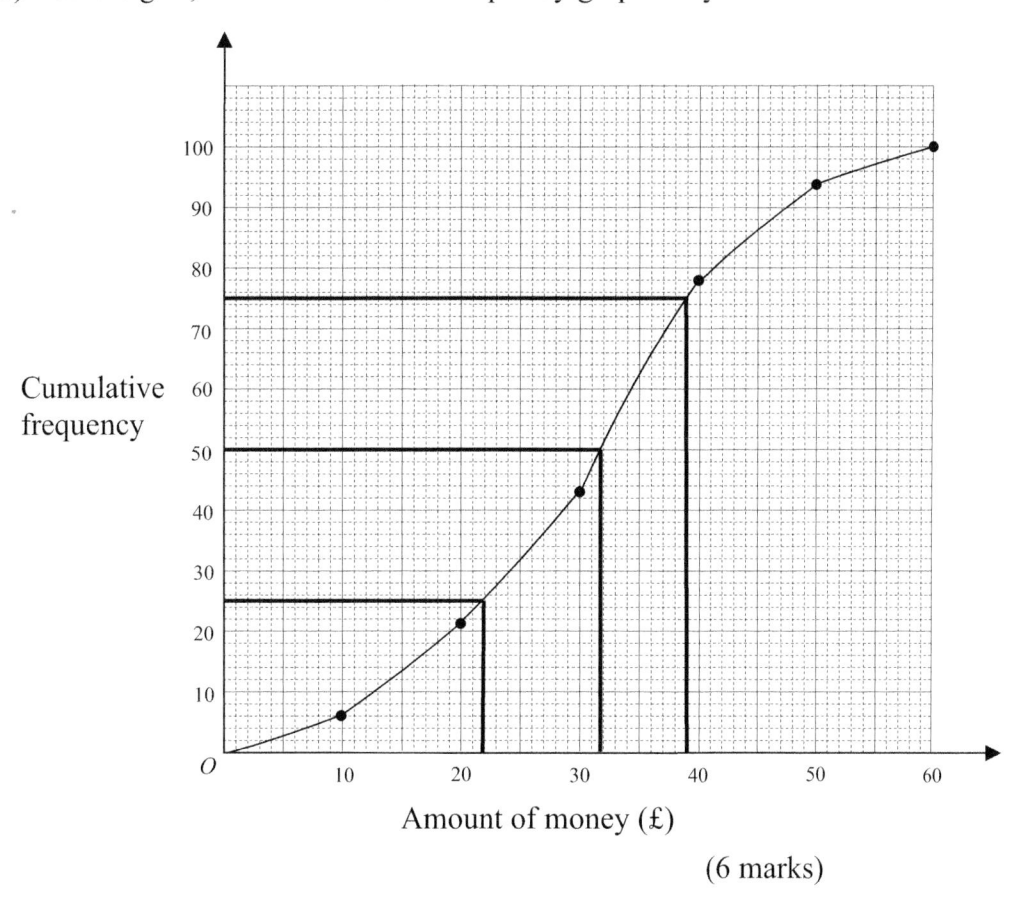

(6 marks)

20(c) Use your graph to complete the table below.

Give your answer to the nearest pound.

Lower quartile (£)	22
Median (£)	32
Upper quartile (£)	39
Interquartile range (£)	17

(4 marks)

21 Jack has 5 black beads, 2 blue beads and 3 red beads in a bag. He takes a bead at random from the bag and put it back. Then he takes the second bead at random from the bag.

21 (a) What is the probability that both beads are red?

The fully probability tree diagram is labelled below.

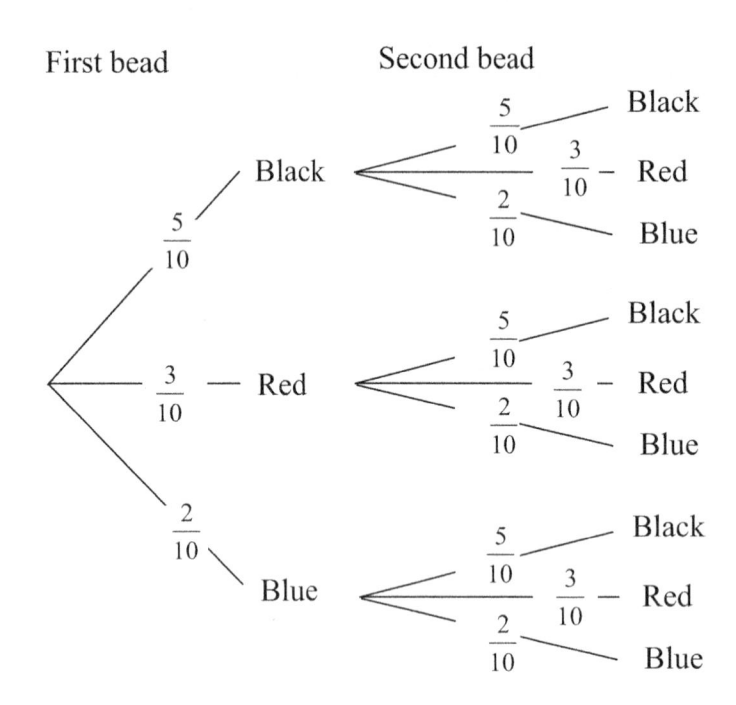

First bead   Second bead

```
           Black  <  5/10 — Black
         /            3/10 — Red
    5/10              2/10 — Blue
       /
      /               5/10 — Black
   — 3/10 — Red   <   3/10 — Red
      \               2/10 — Blue
       \
    2/10              5/10 — Black
         \            
           Blue   <   3/10 — Red
                      2/10 — Blue
```

The probability, that both beads are red, is:

$\dfrac{3}{10} \times \dfrac{3}{10} = \dfrac{9}{100}$

Answer $\dfrac{9}{100}$ (4 marks)

21(b) What is the probability that just one bead is red?

From the fully probability tree diagram above, the probability, that just one bead is red, is:

$\dfrac{5}{10} \times \dfrac{3}{10} + \dfrac{3}{10} \times \dfrac{5}{10} + \dfrac{3}{10} \times \dfrac{2}{10} + \dfrac{2}{10} \times \dfrac{3}{10} = \dfrac{21}{50}$

Answer $\dfrac{21}{50}$ (3 marks)

22 Line *L* passes through (2,1) and (3,3).

Work out the equation of the line.

Give your answer in the form $y = mx + c$.

$y - 3 = \dfrac{3-1}{3-2} \times (x-3) \Rightarrow y - 3 = 2x - 6 \Rightarrow y = 2x - 3$

Answer $y = 2x - 3$ (2 marks)

23 *OAB* is a triangle.

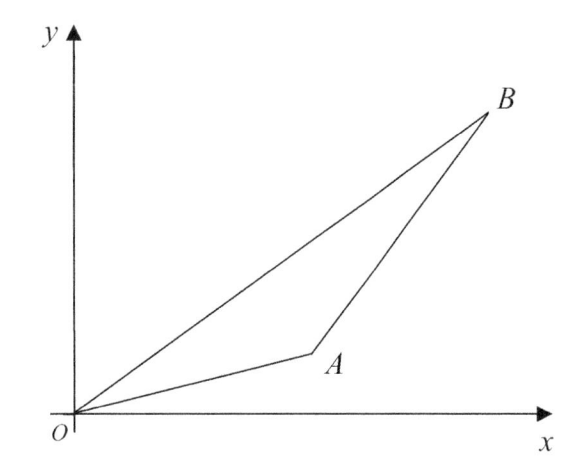

$\vec{OA} = \begin{pmatrix} 4 \\ 1 \end{pmatrix}$, $\vec{OB} = \begin{pmatrix} 7 \\ 5 \end{pmatrix}$

Work out the magnitude of $\vec{AB}$

$\vec{AB} = \vec{OB} - \vec{OA} = \begin{pmatrix} 7 \\ 5 \end{pmatrix} - \begin{pmatrix} 4 \\ 1 \end{pmatrix} = \begin{pmatrix} 3 \\ 4 \end{pmatrix}$

The magnitude of $\vec{AB}$ is $\sqrt{x^2 + y^2} = \sqrt{3^2 + 4^2} = 5$

Answer   5   (3 marks)

24 The diagram shows the graph of $y = \cos x$ for $0° \leq x \leq 360°$

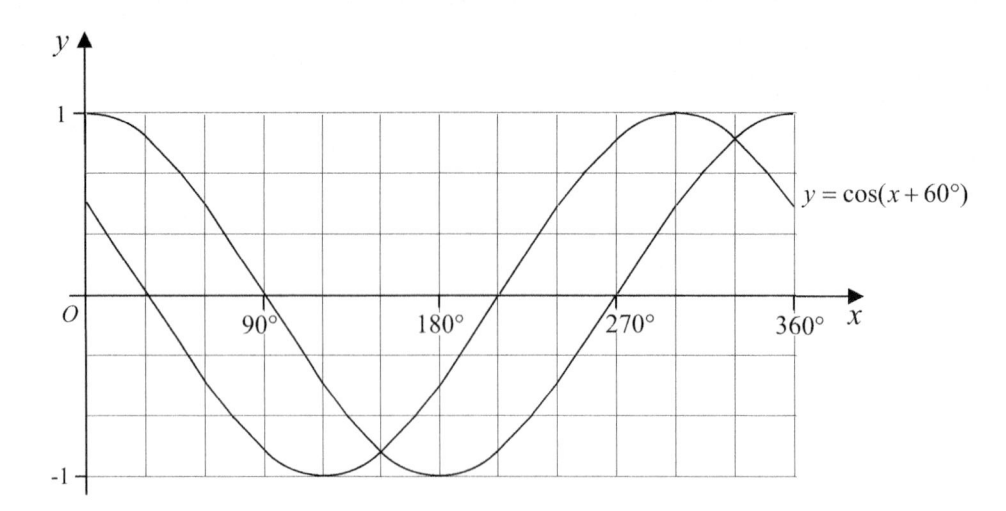

24(a) On the grid above, sketch the graph of $y = \cos(x + 60°)$ for $0° \leq x \leq 360°$

As shown on the graph.

(3 marks)

24(b) The graph of $y = 2\cos(x + 60°) + 1$ has a maximum at point A for $0° \leq x \leq 360°$. Write down the coordinates of A.

$y = \cos(x + 60°)$ has a maximum at $(300°, 1)$, for $0° \leq x \leq 360°$

$\therefore y = 2\cos(x + 60°) + 1$ has a maximum at $(300°, 3)$

The coordinates of A are $(300°, 3)$

Answer $(300°, 3)$ (3 marks)

25   ξ is a universal set.

$n(\xi) = 35$, $n(A) = 8$, $n(B) = 10$, $n(C) = 14$, $n(B \cap C) = 4$, $n(A \cap C) = 3$.

25(a) Complete the Venn diagram to show the number of elements in each region of the Venn diagram.

Firstly fill the number of elements in the following order:

$n(B \cap C) = 4$, $n(A \cap C) = 3$, on the diagram.

Secondly fill the remaining number of elements of sets A, B and C, on the diagram.

$n(A)=8=3+5$, $n(B) = 10=4+6$, $n(C) = 14=3+4+7$

Thirdly fill the remaining number of elements of set ξ, on the diagram.

$n(A \cup B \cup C)=3+7+4+6+5=25$, $n(\xi) = 35= n(A \cup B \cup C)+10$

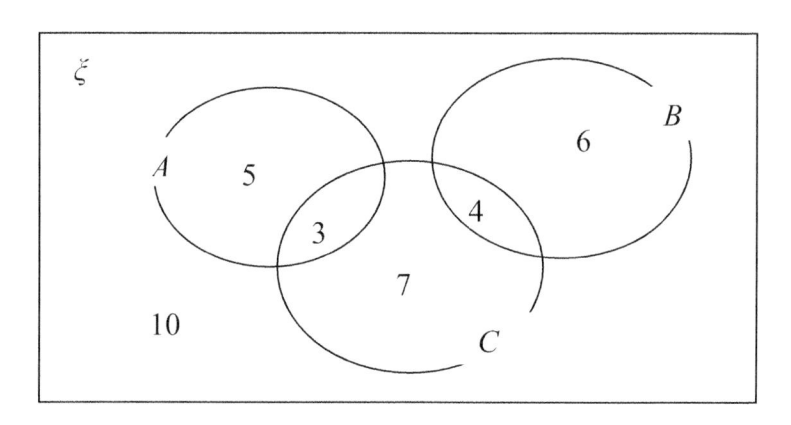

As shown on the Venn diagram   (4 marks)

25(b) Find $n(A \cup C)$

$n(A \cup C) = 5+3+7+4 = 19$

Answer   19   (3 marks)

25(c) Find $n(C \cap B')$

$n(C \cap B') = 3+7 = 10$

Answer   10   (3 marks)

10

113

Printed in Great Britain
by Amazon